Freeway of Love

**JAN
LATIOLAIS-
HARGRAVE**

KENDALL/HUNT PUBLISHING COMPANY
4050 Westmark Drive Dubuque, Iowa 52002

Gender Note: Even though many of the sketches depict female, you may come to the conclusion that this shows an unfair gender bias. This is not the case, the book is meant to be helpful to both men and women. Despite the obvious existence of distinct behavioral patterns and courtship rituals, it should be noted that all human beings are individuals and that every personal interaction is a unique event requiring thoughtful consideration and common sense.

Copyright © 1999 by Hargrave & Associates

ISBN-13 978-0-7872-5312-7

All rights reserved. No part of this publication may be reproduced, stored in a retrieval system, or transmitted, in any form or by any means, electronic, mechanical, photocopying, recording, or otherwise, without the prior written permission of the copyright owner.

Printed in the United States of America

10 9 8 7 6

*To Sheryl, thanks for being my guardian angel,
for teaching me how to tie my shoes and for
holding my hand since first grade.
I "lub" you and couldn't have done it without you!*

*To Glenn, thanks for being my playmate, my protector,
my friend, my love. You are my authentic "gentle man"
who properly and superlatively defines the term, "gentleman."*

*To CeCe. Thanks for reminding me about what
really matters and for teaching me to trust my soul.
How you understand me, even when I'm sitting at the computer
for hours on end, swearing, dressed in my uniform,
with huge goggle-eye glasses on my face and a
gaudy rhinestone "Miss America" crown on my head,
still never ceases to amaze me. What a hero!*

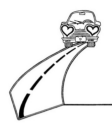

Contents

4 I WANT A MAN WITH A SLOW HAND 63

5 JUST WANT YOUR EXTRA TIME, AND YOUR KISS 95

6 SMOOTH OPERATOR 111

PREFACE

On a quiet street in Santa Barbara lies one of the most charming resting spots in the nation. It's a romantic story-book bed and breakfast nest that serves as home to seasoned couples whose deepest hearts' desire is to insure that the love they've planted will continue to flourish and grow, or to newly-wed honeymooners who arrive carrying a specially wrapped tissue-filled shoe box containing slices of sweet-smelling wedding cake and the bride's precious bouquet. The newly-weds are usually filled with passion and excitement as they "settle down" and hope to spend a joyous life until "death do us part."

Each room at the inn has a romantic flair, smells of lilac and is decorated with delicate curtains, lavish bedspreads and the best mattresses money can buy. The rooms are cozy, fanciful, each houses a whirlpool bath and sounds of romantic melodies ring in the background, while rays of warm sunshine permeate the lace curtains. The most interesting peculiarity, though, are the diaries comprised of personal collections and thoughts from the lucky couples who've had the opportunity to spend loving hours at the hotel, that are strategically placed on tables throughout every room.

While on a business trip, my sponsoring company saw to it that I had the unique opportunity to rest my head for one night at this magical spot. My visit there left me with memories, both happy and sad, as I thought of the blissful times that had been experienced by many of the guests and as I recalled the painful search for love we all encounter in our lives. As I laid down to rest and thumbed through the diaries to read the romantic stories, one in particular struck a cord in my heart. Though it was only words on paper, the connection between the two lovers was so visible, so real; I carry a copy of part of that personal love note with me to this day. It is a mysterious example of the power that symbols and signals have in relaying a message to another. I must share it with you:

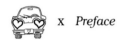

"He is love and in him I am complete.

He is laughter and hope.

He is peace and tranquillity and when we make love all things cease to exist.

He smiles at me, his eyes locked with mine, hands running through my burgundy hair, pulling at me.

A desire to touch, unlike any desire before.

I only laugh louder, cry softer.

I watch him, the man I want to spend an eternity with, making love to me completely.

To my body, to my spirit.

He is truth. We are forever faithfully!"

"Laugh louder, cry softer," words describing pure contentment that each of us should get the opportunity to experience during our life-times. I began to write this book after many years of working with people who expressed to me daily that they felt their, "relationships would be better if there was pure, honest communication," between themselves and their partners. Words do communicate feelings, but the symbols and signals that accompany these words are vehicles that announce the emotions behind such phrases as, "Honey, I'm home," to "I'm wild about you," or "Darling, I adore you," "I'm yours," or even, "I'm sorry."

After speaking with people concerning romantic nonverbal communi-cation, it became apparent to me how little we know about how to achieve the feelings, and experience the consolation that honest love can bring us. We've been taught how to balance a checkbook, stamp out ring around the collar, and put together a gourmet meal, but we've never been taught how to create a trusting, loving relationship.

Love is more than just a feeling, more than a romantic interlude of emotional exhilaration; real love is an array of behaviors, attitudes and in a real sense, true love is a labor of love for it requires us to change our actions; public and private, emotional and spiritual.

Through my spirit of playfulness and joyfulness, I bring to you that special language of romance: sensual body language. Relax and deliver yourself from the bonds of obligation and responsibility and release yourself to a sense of delight as we travel on the *Freeway of Love*. In a lively manner, I've tried to help you rekindle the sense of young love, passion and romance that you've perhaps buried deep inside.

"Music moves the body, but lyrics move the soul!" In my search to combine music and movement to lyrics and thoughts, I've chosen well-known hits containing rhythmical beats to move your body. While at the same time, it is my hope that thoughtful consideration of the message contained in each song will float through your mind as you read and savor each segment of the book.

Why connect travel with love? The correlation was too astonishing. From obtaining a driver's license to following the directive signals and signs along the roadsides of America, the experiences along the highway to romantic love were so coincidental and parallel to driving, that I just couldn't resist it. From the types of cars we drive, the suggestive license plates we desire, to the sensual wording of warning road messages (Dangerous Curves Ahead, Soft Shoulders) we observe while driving; there is suggestive love talk all around town.

Years ago, I, too, had a rather suggestive license plate. Mine read FONDA-U. Probably my mind was preparing me for this book, even back then. I continue to search the highways today for traffic signs that can translate to love signals and for license plates that play with the language of love. What are some that you've seen? I've come across these and many more:

UQT-PIE

U.S. MALE

LOV-R-BOY

IMZ14U

SPO-KN4

2DI4

One of the best things about being an adult is that you can include romance as part of your playing. Having fun with the person you love is the premier form of play as it provides you with the opportunity to

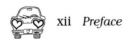

have a totally carefree experience (and sometimes mind-altering view) of your lover. For when we do play, we are most precisely ourselves.

Playing together—whether you play house, play yard, play sports, play dress-up-and-go-out, or play doctor—always doubles the fun because you feel not only the pleasure of your partner's company, but the incredible pleasure of laughter and joy in your life. Therefore, have fun with the book and watch for the signs of love as you drive; they're unbelievable!

Play well. Play hard. Play on. Play often. Play for keeps.

INTRODUCTION

He's sitting across the aisle, ahead of you in line, or reading the newspaper at the next table. You can't stop staring at him and you have a gut feeling that this is the man of your dreams. Problem is, if you don't do something pronto, he's going to walk right out of your life forever. What to do?

Read the signals. Body language speaks volumes. Just smile warmly, look into his eyes, and make it painfully obvious that you're looking for an excuse to talk to him. If he doesn't take the hint and come over, keep looking in his direction, run your hands through your hair and continue flashing a smile at him at every opportunity. Leave him in no doubt that the freeway is clear and that he has the green light to come over and talk.

Can't imagine having the guts to pull off the above scenario? It does take courage and thick skin to approach a complete stranger when he's least expecting it. The rejection factor is high.

Developing a comprehensive knowledge of nonverbal courtship gestures, can help you determine the meaning and intention of a stranger's smile from a far away table, a person's sneaking glance from across a crowded room, or an acquaintance's accidental touch beneath a business table.

This book is to help you understand sexual body language by awakening your instinctive knowledge about human nature that lies dominant in your subconscious. We signal a dozen messages without words for every idea that is delivered in spoken language.

It is a complicated business: Mario Pei claims to have identified 700,000 different human nonverbal signals and noted researcher, M. H. Krout, reported 5,000 individual hand gestures alone. This book specializes in the body language secrets of attraction and courtship, and is designed to help you to greater success in your search for love.

After reading it, with patience and practice, you'll be able to tell if another person is available for a potential encounter: if they are interested in talking with you, dancing with you or even kissing you.

Understand the secrets of sexual body language and quickly you will know far more about what other people are thinking—thoughts they may or may not wish you to know; feelings they may not yet have consciously realized for themselves.

This book has been written for anyone, single or married, who wants to know how to create and sustain a vibrant, deeply rewarding love relationship. The nonverbal secrets you will learn can help you to revitalize a long-term relationship, as well as deepen the intimacy of a new romance. Throughout the book there are specific exercises to help you apply what you have learned and to make your relationship stronger. A lasting relationship doesn't just happen; you create it.

Turn-on Signals While Traveling on the Freeway of Love is a comprehensive study of nonverbal sexual communication. It will explain how to understand, create and control powerful sensual signals and reveal to you ways you can use body talk to find a partner and develop a relationship, from first glances through to greater intimacy.

The early stages of courtship are crucial and in many ways the most challenging, but they are also the most exciting. Ahead may lie the relationship of a lifetime and it is body talk that supports us in the first process of "checking out" the intended partner. Therefore, mastering unspoken signals can greatly improve your chances for a romantic connection to develop.

Chapter One begins by looking at first impressions and how important they are. It will reveal to you keys to determine who is available and who is not; what and whom we find attractive and why; and what we do to enhance our best assets. It will help you to ascertain your flirting profile and lastly, it leads you through creating your own Lovemap; the essential requirement for selecting the perfect Dream Lover for you.

Chapter Two examines how a person's eyes play a crucial role in the first encounter between two people. The eyes are described as Cupid's Arrows in this chapter and information concerning staring, gazing, and winking is examined in detail. The emotions of the face are analyzed as well as the various smiles seen on the faces of people involved in first encounters. Chapter Two also includes a test for the reader to determine the romantic style he uses during courtship.

In Chapter Three the emphasis is on moving to greater intimacy. This chapter deals with personal space and space invasion. It includes signs of sexual interest displayed by men and by women as they approach each other, as they pass by each other, and it fully explains the concept of body blocks. Space invasion with bodies, as well as with objects is discussed in detail and the proverbial, "does 'no' ever mean 'yes,'" is finally answered.

Chapter Four examines sensitive, seductive, soothing touching between partners. It includes a Love Language test to determine both you and your partner's dominant sense for communicating with others, not only in affairs of the heart, but also in everyday life. A palm-reading exercise, to check on the number of marriages and children you or your partner may have, is near the end and proves to be quite enlightening.

Chapter Five begins a grand tour of the body from the redness of the lips to tips of the toes, showing how every bit of your body expresses your thoughts and desires. Chapter Six holds a special section on honesty and dishonesty and the give-away signals that help us sort the truth tellers from the liars. Finally the book looks at the world of complex gesture clusters, what we find most in real-life encounters, where people send numerous individual nonverbal communications simultaneously. By the last chapter, you will know an infinite number of secrets about the body language of attraction and how to interpret these signals to your advantage in your search for love and sex.

Are you tired of waiting for the man or woman you're nuts about to say "I love you?" Here's hope: He or she may already be saying it. Men and women have carefully used the art of nonverbal communication for centuries and have developed hundreds of ways to express those three little words without having actually to resort to verbalizing them, but few men and women have put a label to these signals.

Here for the first time, the inaudible but unmistakable signs that a guy's in lo . . . . . well, that they . . . . . um, you know, feel very strongly about . . . . . oooooh, you get the picture, will be revealed. Let's first examine several differences between the various levels of love, as in, "loves me, loves me not."

HE LOVES YOU ...

. . . if he's interested in your entire life, your goals, your dreams.

. . . if he thinks you're beautiful in the morning.

. . . if he considers your feelings about important issues.

. . . if he puts on an apron and makes you spaghetti.

. . . if he always finds you just the right present.

. . . if he calls your answering machine just to hear your voice.

. . . if his lovemaking concerns your satisfaction as well as his.

. . . if he brings you soup when you're ill.

. . . (but you'll never know it) if he watches you while you sleep.

HE LOVES YOU NOT ...

. . . if he makes passes at your girlfriends.

. . . if he completely forgets your birthday or Valentine's Day.

. . . if you start to recognize his "moves."

. . . if he takes you for granted.

. . . if he always puts his friends before you.

Although all of the above were written about men, the information here and throughout the book, also applies to women. Until one is 100 percent sure, though, he's in love, he might use phrases like those below:

LIKE YOU ...

"Luv ya, babe."

"You're the best."

"You're an angel."

"You're amazing."

"You mean so much to me."

"You're my last girlfriend/boyfriend."

GETTING CLOSER ...

"I need you."

"I really care about you."

"I can't imagine life without you."

"Where have you been all my life?"

"I really, really enjoy your company."

LOVE ...

"I love you."

The information I've included for you in this book will allow you to determine a person's feelings for you long before they speak the words of love.

You will be able to understand why men seem so hopeless at picking up apparently clear signals of "yes" or "no" or "I haven't decided yet" and why a woman who is really interested in a man, may: a) avoid him like the plague, b) look away every time he smiles at her, or c) hardly eat anything at all the first time he takes her for a feast at his favorite restaurant.

Travel the "freeway of love" with me to better understand the sexual turn-on signals for true love: love that lasts, love that heals, love that transforms, and love that brings inestimable joy. Let's get it on!

Let's Get It On

◆B ODIES

Some
bodies are
made for bathing
suits, others look
best in formals.
Some bodies
are made
for
very tight pants,
while others look best
in long, full skirts. Some
bodies are made
for mannish
suits, others
look best
in
frilly blouses.
Some bodies are made
for hats and gloves, while
others look great in jeans.
Some bodies are made for
eyelet lace, while some
need 100% cotton.
Some bodies are
made for trends
and fashion,
mine is
made
for love!

MUSIC MOVES THE BODY, LYRICS MOVE THE SOUL

It has taken me many years, a lot of pain, and a great deal of prayer to feel worthy of love. I'm certain there's been no expression in my life that's been more difficult to feel, offer, or accept than love—of myself and others. I know I'm not unusual. Loving ourselves and others is a struggle for most of us. And, like you, I have desperately wanted to love and be loved, certain that if I "knew" love fully, I'd be forever secure and serene.

My search for love is deeply rooted in my childhood. I still remember how I looked, regularly, into the faces of my parents, friends, brother and sister for signs of approval, acceptance and friendship. Any warm expression on their faces meant I was worthy, at that moment, of love. But once the moment passed, I never trusted that I was still worthy, and so I felt compelled to search some more, again and again and again.

What I made great efforts for as a child and what I still forget as an adult is that I am loved and fully worthy of love, and that my very existence is proof. I am now and always have been part of the spiritual universe. Our worthiness should be unquestionable! Happiness is our birthright so long as we live fully and love truly.

In my personal search for love, I grasped men and possessions, achievements and "causes," before I came to know where love had resided all the time. Still today, though, frequent reminders and daily moments of reflection are necessary for me to know that real love lies deep within my center and has endless dimensions. Sometimes love is joy. Sometimes passion. Sometimes moments of serenity amongst the laughter and sadness. Sometimes it's when I'm lonesome. Generally love is soft. But it also may sting. Love is forever changing and takes real courage.

All that love is, there's much it is not. Love is not shaming. Nor is it punishing. Love does not criticize, degrade, or diminish; it frees and praises. It makes friends of strangers, softens our rough edges and strengthens our assets.

I wrote this book on finding love because I believe that all of us share the same struggles with self-knowledge. We must all know that love's home is within each of us. Finding the courage to be honest and vulnerable with our fellow travelers, whose lives mirror our own and from whom we desire love, helps us to remember our importance, and theirs.

I've often been helped across a rough road, over a bumpy path, through a detour, or down an unfamiliar avenue by reading a few thoughtful lines or listening to a friend's well-chosen words. I hope what you read here will serve you in your search for love, as others' words and a deeper understanding into myself have helped me in my search. Looking for love isn't easy. The irony is that the harder we look for love, the more blurred is our vision. Only when we become quiet, trust that we are worthy and know that love is our birthright, do we discover that when love is real, we see it with our hearts.

The question eternally whispering around our souls is, "Do I dare let you in, to share my space, to know my heart's longing, to feel my fears?" Only when we trust to say "yes" will we find the peace for which our souls long.

Destiny has its own course in each of our lives. As we travel the "freeway of love," we must remember that our interactions with others who are special will thankfully be parallel at times. However, our paths will sharply intersect now and then and we'll even find ourselves at painful crossroads on occasion. The challenges of a rough passage only confront us when it's time to grow. What we must understand is that the journey, alone or in partnership, will be uphill at least half of the time. But we must also believe the path will only be as rugged as it needs to be to ensure our fullest development.

Love creates music, it provides harmony like a song of happiness that emerges from our hearts. Celebrate your partner's avenue to fulfillment, feel joy when your paths are parallel and trust that you are only in a growth process when your directions seem at crossroads. I have chosen to begin each chapter with well known song titles that are predominately tender and romantic. Since music moves the body and lyrics move the soul; the rhythm, spirit, and movement you begin to feel when you recall each song should trigger memories and fantasies within you. Your enjoyment and fulfillment of each chapter lies in your ability to mentally build intimacy in your heart and make the scenes come alive.

Whatever your destination, take the scenic route. Learn to read the signals, the warning signs, and the markers. Observing these guides can help you avoid detours, alert you to hazardous conditions which

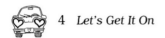

lie immediately ahead and make your trip on the "freeway of love," or highway to happiness, more pleasant and more enjoyable.

ENTERING THE TUNNEL OF LOVE

On a highway or in a crowded room, you experience a glance, a smile, a wink. Is it an exciting flirtatious "come-on" or just an over-friendly gesture? Learning how to send, understand, create and control powerful sexual signals can help improve your chances of developing a loving, lasting relationship or make your passage smoother to keep you surrounded by admirers until you find one that is right for you.

In human relationships, it is never the words that really count. They are, in the deepest sense, unimportant because they create only seven percent of our communication. The other 93 percent is body talk, the body language of posture, gesture and expression with which we communicate what we really mean.

In intimate relationships, we are unavoidably drawn into using our bodies to communicate even more fully than usual. We move closer and converse through touch; we listen and learn through the sound of a heartbeat and of breathing, and we analyze men and women from head to toe to decode the messages sent by each body part.

Since so much body talk happens at an unconscious level, with signals beyond both our awareness and our control, we need to become fully conscious of these signs if we are to use them successfully.

As with any language, sexual body talk has its letters of the alphabet, individual elements that we must know if we are to be literate. From first glances through greater intimacy, careful observation of body talk gives us numerous clues to our own or a loved one's true feelings.

We humans are such sexual beings. Intimacy is a principal motivator in our lives and often occupies a great amount of our thinking time while awake, day-dreaming, and even in our dreams while we're asleep. Many people make mistakes in their search for love much of the time, these failures and often heartbreaking misunderstandings usually occur because we fail to comprehend or perhaps even think about the nonverbal signals we're sending to others and receiving back from those around us.

It is possible to change, but it may require some uncomfortable self-searching in order to increase your self-awareness, and ultimately improve your self-confidence. In addition, it will take some committed hard work, both at home and out in the "research field" with other people, to properly study this subject and develop new "reading skills" with sensitivity, accuracy and sincerity.

The nonverbal language of attraction involves all our senses. We scan each other's eyes, facial expressions and body postures for clues to personality, mood, attractiveness, flirtation levels and signals of intent. We are acutely aware of the proximity of the other person to us. We are aware of their scent and they are of ours. We listen intently to the sound of their voice, not just their words. In some cases we desperately want to touch them, to hold them, to kiss them.

To slow down, to yield or to come to a complete stop are signs we observe as we travel the highways of life. Understanding the secrets and signals of sexual body language will allow you to drive down lover's lane on cruise control. It is your radar to determine how far, how fast, and how turned-on another is to you and by you.

Who is available and who is not? We need, at the start of any relationship, to gauge whether it is worth going ahead or to come to a halt with our intentions. Putting your best foot forward to encourage a new relationship begins with being friendly and warm. It's foolish to try to impress, or to make yourself into a sexual image, or to learn the right phrases. None of these work. The enduring trait, the one thing that everyone agrees on is friendliness. If you are friendly and warm, no one sees that as anything less than perfection.

◆B UCKLE UP AND ENJOY THE RIDE

Since playfulness is one of the core elements of friendliness, flirting is at the heart of romance. Maybe extending friendship is a major part of flirting, but somehow when that friendliness comes from a person we're attracted to, it explodes into something more special. It's a little bit naughty and can be quite a challenge.

Everyone has the ability to flirt. As little children, we do it naturally. Unfortunately, all that charm, grace, and whimsy usually gets lost somewhere along the path to adulthood. Somehow, we forgot that flirting is as simple as getting along with others, enthralling them with our sensuality and attractiveness, our humor and our common sense.

Since flirting is child's play, all you have to do is unearth the treasures in your own personality, by rediscovering all those alluring traits you've been suppressing. It's putting the childlike qualities of love, life, trust, hand holding and romance back into your life. With this casual, whimsical, and mischievous spirit, you'll succeed at bringing out your own openness and sincerity, as well as that of a new companion.

To flirt, you've got to dredge up the little boy or girl inside you, the one who's been neglected by your drive for success. And when you discover that four- or five-year-old, give that person some freedom. Imagine yourself at a birthday party when you were eight. Think of the fun you had at summer camp when you played spin-the-bottle. Try to recreate that *"joie de vivre"* (joy of life), and you'll magnify your allure.

Because flirting is as much an attitude as it is a set of actions, how you think about it is as important as how you do it. You need delicacy, patience, confidence and a keen observation of others and yourself. Keep reminding yourself that by flirting, you are doing someone a favor, since you are opening the lines of communication.

To sharpen your flirting profile, just unearth the treasures in your own personality. The more you develop, improve and understand your flirtatious assets, the sooner you can reap the benefits of flirting. Certain gestures, actions, looks and touches will bring out the best in you. Which ones are they? By recognizing your own flirting style, and what type of person you get the most flirting pleasure from, you put your flirtatious moments to best use. Try the following quiz to assess how fluent you are in the area of flirting and sensual nonverbal communication.

YOUR FLIRTING PROFILE

1. You're meeting a friend at happy hour, and she's late. You:
   a. Keep your head down; you don't need every slimeball in the place chatting with you.
   b. Get a drink and share a few jokes with the bartender.
   c. Perch sexually on your bar stool, run your hands through your hair, and scope out the place.

2. You dress to:
   a. Cover your nakedness.

b. Accentuate the positive.

c. Impress.

3. Possible dating partners enjoy compliments about:

   a. Their good looks.

   b. Their personal qualities.

   c. Their desirable bodies.

4. How much time, money, and energy do you spend on your appearance?

   a. Minimal; just the basics.

   b. A fair amount; work out regularly, follow fashion and feel well put together.

   c. Tons; total gym bunny, bags are packed right now!

5. You're at a comedy club and you're dragged on stage to participate in a silly routine. You:

   a. Are totally embarrassed in front of all of those people and giggle the entire time.

   b. Roll with it, even though you know you look a little stupid.

   c. Take over the entire act; this is your time to shine.

6. At a party, you're gabbing with a group when a person you have been trying to attract enters the conversational circle. You:

   a. Clamp up.

   b. Gradually included him/her into the conversation.

   c. Become more animated and funny.

7. It's your first date with someone, and when asked what you prefer doing, you answer:

   a. "Whatever you want to do."

   b. "Well, I'd love to X, Y, or Z. Do you have any other ideas?"

   c. "You know, I'm up for almost anything," followed by a suggestive stare.

8. Once you spot someone you are interested in, you:

   a. Avoid eye contact; it's too nerve wracking.

   b. Play peek-a-boo for a few seconds, then make direct eye contact.

c. Use exciting, thunderbolt eye contact from the onset to make certain that you're noticed.

9. After you've initiated conversation, a sure signal that he or she thinks you're a doofus, and doesn't want to continue talking might be:

a. Avoiding eye contact with you.

b. Crossing his arms across his chest.

c. Turning his body away from you.

10. Once you've read signals that someone across the room is interested, to keep up that interest, you should:

a. Back off: take your focus totally off formally flirtatious behavior for a few minutes.

b. Play with a piece of your clothing, twirl your drink, twist an earring, or caress a set of keys.

c. Hike your skirt to expose your leg, if you're female; tuck your thumbs into your belt loops and spread your fingers around your zipper area, if you're male.

11. To seal the deal, once they are near you and communication begins, you:

a. Cling and monopolize "your new honey" all evening.

b. Accidentally brush his/her forearm while telling a funny story.

c. Create a nickname for your new friend as a stepping-stone to intimacy.

12. The most flirtatious part of the hand is the:

a. Fingers

b. Thumb

c. Wrist

13. While driving in traffic day after day, you see a special person you want to attract at the same hour each day. Casual glances have been made, but you want to take flirting one step further, you should:

a. Plan a simultaneous stop at the traffic light and attempt to start a conversation.

b. Place a sign on your car rear window announcing the sale of your car for a ridiculously low figure.

    c. Fake roadside car trouble and display provocative body language to get help.

14. Flowers given at the beginning of a relationship:

    a. Often pressure a woman.

    b. Are best given one at a time.

    c. Should always come by the dozens.

15. As men loosen their ties at the end of a romantic evening, in a flirtatious gesture, women:

    a. Feel they appear sloppy.

    b. Want them to also remove their jackets.

    c. Hope that they can't keep the rest of their clothes on a minute longer.

16. The most flirtatious way to leave a room is to:

    a. Make a point to say good-bye to everyone.

    b. Thank the host.

    c. Rush out, you have someplace else to go.

17. Flirts, while driving:

    a. Wave shyly to good looking people.

    b. Wave to everyone.

    c. Use tasteless hand signals.

18. To arouse the attention of an attractive person walking a dog, you would:

    a. Comment on the dog.

    b. Begin to talk to the dog.

    c. Wink and smile coyly towards the attractive person.

19. Flirtatious conversations:

    a. Usually start off as tongue-tied.

    b. Are always in the present tense.

    c. Are accompanied by flirtatious gestures.

20. The best way to flirt while enjoying a liquid refreshment is to:

    a. Order a drink that comes with an umbrella.

    b. Order a drink that comes with a straw.

    c. Order a shot of anything.

21. The best advice to help create a flirtatious home environment:

   a. Is to keep your apartment on the warm side.

   b. Is to have silly books or games on the coffee table.

   c. Is to have a bar set up in the living room.

SCORING:

Mostly A's:

You took this test thinking it was about *fishing* not *flirting*. Just kidding! You're smart enough to know that flirting can help you, but too scared to try. Get out there; go places where you know you can have fun. If you're doing things you enjoy, you can't help but give off inviting vibes.

Mostly B's:

You're confident about yourself, your sexuality, and your attractiveness. You may not be a perfect specimen, but you've got the perfect mix of inviting and interesting characteristics. You seek out what makes you laugh with a vengeance, and you ooze sexuality.

Mostly C's:

Whoa! You're begging for it. There are certain types of people who find way-out-there individuals attractive, but if you're looking for more than a string of short-term affairs, you need to tone it down a touch. There is such a thing as "trying too hard," and that puts people off.

Whether you're a shy beginner or an advanced seducer, the tips that follow will soon have you charming the socks off of everyone.

TTRACTION'S TELL-TALE SIGNS

The first steps of a relationship are in many ways the most challenging, but also the most exciting. We have to take a risk, to approach or allow an approach at the beginning, when we are not close enough for words and rely entirely on body talk to make contact. Understanding sexual body talk helps you to determine what the other person is thinking or feeling. It also signals the direction in which another person is moving, whether it's towards you or away from you.

During these precious first few minutes, we're checking whether we like the other person and whether he or she likes us. At various points along the road we can withdraw, or be rejected. We may find that we have nothing in common and decide to go our separate ways at an early stage, or we may move closer and closer, until eventually our choice is made, and we've found someone who truly interests us.

Once we spot someone we want to attract, we begin to behave as primitive animals do; we show ourselves off to our best advantage. Like the peacock who preens, we flutter our plumes and display our attractions. Preening is vital, not only because it makes us look desirable, but also because it signals to the other person that we are interested, an irresistible message.

A woman, while preening, smoothes her hair into place, licks her lips to make them more inviting, sways her hips a little more than usual, straightens her back and even sucks in her stomach. Women also will unconsciously adjust a belt, tug at their skirt length or slowly cross and uncross their legs to draw attention to themselves.

Men preen by straightening their ties, adjusting their shirt cuffs, running their hands through their hair, thrusting out their chests, or sometimes will stand with their thumbs tucked inside their belt loops. Both men and women, when displaying sexual body language, will touch themselves far more than normal to remind whoever is watching of the delights of touching, particularly how wonderful it would feel if the interested party touched them.

There's attractive, there's beautiful, and there's even traffic-stopping stunning. The question of what we find attractive in others and what we do to enhance our own best assets is a major preoccupation during at least some part of our lives. We have a never-ending desire for love and to be loved. How we set about searching for another person to love and be loved, often occupies much of our thinking time while awake, day-dreaming, and even in our dreams while asleep.

Each of us has our own mental picture of what we feel is the "perfect lover/mate," from looks to personality. What are the turn-ons? Some are physical characteristics; some are psychological. Either way, there's something special that makes us want to get to know the other person better.

The success that people have in sexual encounters with members of the opposite sex is directly related to their ability to send courtship signals and to recognize those being sent back. Women, much more than men, are aware of the nonverbal signals that communicate desire for involvement.

During a couple's first contact, it has been noted that men tend to scan a woman's body completely first, then return their gaze to her face. Women, on the other hand, concentrate on lips and eyes.

The first nonverbal judgment of another is an appearance inventory. Height may be important; women like their men taller than themselves, but men are wary of taller women, whom they often judge as dominating.

Slim is currently seen as attractive by both sexes. Psychologist W. H. Sheldon identifies three body types. The elegant ectomorph shape (tall and thin) is, he claims, the sign of a quiet, stubborn and ambitious personality. The wide-shouldered mesomorph shape (wide upper body and slender hips) is known to be adventurous and self-reliant. The pear-shaped endomorph (slender shoulders and wide hip area) is indicative of a warm, talkative, and trusting personality.

WHAT'S MY LINE?

We must first keep in mind that the clothes we wear make a loud non-verbal statement about who we are, what we stand for, where we work, how much we care about our appearance and fashion trends, and how interested we are in displaying our sexuality. Once again, we are faced with a dilemma: dressing very provocatively, especially in the case of women, is likely to attract a great deal of sexual attention.

The more overtly sexual clothing is, the more members of the opposite gender will be aroused, but arousal is not the same as attraction. Arousal might be the effect you desire, but consider the likely detrimental side-effects. What will people of the same sex think of you? Will they feel threatened by your flaunted sexuality? Will people take you for a teaser?

The colors of our clothes speak volumes. The "hot" colors, especially scarlet, are all linked with sexuality. Bright red actually makes us physically aroused; our breathing and heart rates rise in the presence of strong colors. Other colors carry significant nonverbal messages.

Soft colors, such as white or pink, cause subdued behavior from those around you. How does the color black make you feel? The color yellow? The color purple? Be aware of how each color makes you feel and use this to determine what effect each color may have on someone you want to attract.

Our imaginations play a central role in the early formation of relationships. One of the greatest "turn-ons" is imagining the parts of another person's body that we cannot see. Clothes that hint at what lies below the folds of material are much more exciting than show-it-all displays in short skirts or shirts unbuttoned to the waist. A woman wearing a long skirt with a discreet split, that occasionally reveals a flash of leg, is infinitely alluring. In the same way, men's clothes that suggest a fine body are usually sexier to women than skin-tight T-shirts and spray-on jeans.

Prior to the exchange of verbal information, there will be many other nonverbal clues to the status and personality of the person to whom you are attracted. Wedding rings, diamond rings, watches and even shoes are all nonverbal indicators. The latter say a great deal about us because they are at the border of our bodies, but they often receive the least care. How high or low are the heels? How clean are the shoes? How well made? How fashionable or traditional? Good-quality, well-made shoes are always a sign of high status, and the possession of high status enhances our sexual attraction.

◆S HOW US SOME IDENTIFICATION— THE SYMBOLISM OF CARS

For as long as they have existed, cars have been used as status symbols. A car serves as an extension of personal space (and sometimes the ego too), but many people don't realize that getting into someone's car is quite an intimate encroachment on the car-owner's space and also a sacrifice of their own space.

Cars provide an interesting sexual stage as the physical space boundaries are fixed. For example, in the erotic film, *The Lover*, a scene takes place in the back of a car. The man inches his hand towards the young woman's hand in minute movements, until at last their fingers touch. As their hands intertwine both of them are looking out of their respective windows, yet from the sensuality of their touch, it is obvious that they will inevitably become lovers.

Of course, the front seats of cars are where most of the action takes place between courting couples. Driving provides plenty of opportunity for touching "accidentally on purpose." The passenger has the advantage over the driver in that he or she can position him or herself to face towards the driver, lean into the driver's personal space, in a way the driver cannot reciprocate—at least, not without driving dangerously!

Cars do serve as status symbols, but you sometimes don't need a license plate to know someone's hometown. Here's a handy, comical checklist to identify a driver's city or state of origin at a glance.

One hand on wheel, one hand on the horn	New York
One hand on wheel, one fist out the window	Chicago
One hand on wheel, one hand on newspaper, Wellesley sticker on rear window, accelerator to the floor	Boston
One hand on wheel, one hand on cell phone, gun in lap	Los Angeles
Both hands on wheel, eyes shut, both feet on brake	Iowan in Detroit
Both hands in air, both feet on accelerator, head turned to talk to someone in back seat	Rome
One knee on wheel, one hand on crossword puzzle, one hand on latte	Seattle
One hand on hunting knife, one hand holding bar-b-que rib, driving along shoulder of highway	Texas
Sixty-foot limo with hot tub trailer, "just married" painted on back window, green ostrich-skin cowboy boots sticking out of sunroof, radio blaring	Las Vegas
Shotgun in rear window, beer cans on floor, Labrador retriever in pickup bed	Louisiana
One hand tying fishing lines, one hand scraping mosquitoes off windshield, dead deer on roof	Wisconsin

One hand displaying the peace sign, one hand
   holding cup of aged wine from nearby winery,
   bicycle rack attached to rear bumper   San Francisco

One hand on rear-view mirror, one hand on can
   of hair spray, one knee on steering wheel   Hollywood

One hand on wheel, one sun-tanned hand
   clutching exotic orange-blend drink, eyes ogling
   curvaceous bikini-clad models speeding by
   on roller blades   South Beach

One hand on wheel, one hand on CB radio,
   eyes scanning numerous gray-clouded
   smoke stacks   Tennessee

ONFIDENCE, POWER AND STATUS

"He's so fine." "His power is impressive." "The way his eyes sparkle."
"I love his energy." "He looks great in those jeans." "He seems to have
a great sense of humor." "She has great legs." "Her laugh is conta-
gious." "Small waists, big hips, make me crazy." "I'm impressed by
her intelligence." "She's feisty." These are just a few of the comments
made by men and women when asked what makes another downright
attractive.

Think about it: Whether you're in a night club, a grocery store or a
restaurant, and you spot someone who floats your boat, the odds are
that you'll only have one, maybe two shots to connect with each other.
Knowing how to make the best of those short moments is key to your
success in building a relationship.

Like it or not, status is a reliable predictor of sexual attraction. This is
why first impressions are so important. Apart from the obvious symbols of status such as clothing and accessories, an impression of power
can be created by a combination of the way we use our eyes, how comfortable we look in our bodies, how relaxed our faces appear and the
degree to which our muscle tone looks firm and well-shaped.

Our body language reflects the way we feel about ourselves. The higher
our self-esteem, the more comfortable we look in our bodies and the
more attractive we become. The more you like yourself, the more you

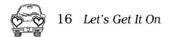

will wear your body around you in comfort. The more comfortable you look, the more attractive you will be to others. When we feel good about ourselves, we tend to hold ourselves upright, balanced and tall.

SEX APPEAL/TURN-ONS

Goodness knows, every man or woman I've ever known has had a completely different view about what is sexy. One woman put it pointedly: "What's sexy? That's easy. If he thinks he's sexy, he's sexy." When women were asked at random the same question, the answer was almost always the same. The single most attractive thing about a man is self-assurance. This should not come as a complete surprise, because when men were asked this same question, they too, repeatedly put self-confidence as one of their highest desirable attributes in women.

What are turn-ons? Some are physical characteristics; some are psychological. The top five turn-ons for men and women are:

Women rank:

1. Eyes (They look here for warmth, sincerity, inner confidence.)

2. Good looks

3. Muscular body

4. Sense of humor

5. Power

Men rank turn-ons in this order:

1. Good looks

2. Sexy body

3. Intelligence

4. Sense of humor

5. Her walk, her stance, the way she sits and flirts

What we're looking for in a man or a woman is imprinted on our subconscious. Psychologist John Money, Ph.D., named the imprint our "Love Map." Others refer to it as our Dream Lover.

This imprint, unique for each of us, defines all the characteristics of our ideal mate. It's composed of everything from the sound of the voice, color of the hair, to the types of activities and scenarios we find pleasant, enjoyable, and erotic. It's called fantasy and much of it is implanted in our minds by the time we are seven years old.

◆F OLLOWING YOUR LOVE MAP TO FIND YOUR DREAM LOVER

Fantasy or not, conscious or not, we tend to gauge every possible relationship by how closely the intended person follows or fits the concept of our Dream Lover. If the Dream Lover you've been involved with has only created nightmares for you, or you already have someone special in your life, but want to feel closer and more loving and aren't quite sure how, the following exercise can rekindle your hope and guide your heart toward love that is healthy, joyous and real.

It is not by accident, nor because of our bad luck that we've ended up with the partners we've had. Rather, it is due to our emotional programming. A person's emotional programming consists of the decisions and beliefs he's made about himself, others, and the world in general while growing up. Each day we're alive, we collect experiences. These unique experiences help us form decisions about ourselves, about people, and about life. It is the combination of all these decisions, our emotional programming, that cause us to make certain choices throughout our adult life; love choices included.

Here's something else to be aware of: The majority of this emotional programming occurs when we're still very young. Psychologists estimate that between birth and eight years of age, we are 80 percent programmed, psychologically. In other words, by the age of eight, 80 percent of our decisions about ourselves and others have already been made.

Accepting and understanding your own emotional programming, why you behave the way you do, is instrumental in discovering the ideal partner for you. Therefore, while completing the following exercise, keep in mind the realizations and insights you'll discover about yourself. During this enlightening process, you'll learn much about the qualities—physical, emotional, mental—that you expect and require for stimulating and satisfactory relationships.

How do you discover your Love Map/Dream Lover? Easy, you'll do some amateur self-psychoanalysis now, wherever you are. It will help you sort the past and figure out what worked and why, as well as what didn't and why. Be prepared for these exercises to unleash long-suppressed or forgotten fantasies and memories. Here's how to proceed:

1. Recall three of your boy-girl interactions between ages five and eight.

2. During those early years, who made you feel comfortable? Who turned you off? And why?

3. Chronologically list the name of each partner you've had a significant relationship with, including the one you are with now. Include anyone to whom you were very emotionally attached.

4. Give each partner a page. Put his or her name at the top and then think about and answer the following questions:

   a. Where did we meet?

   b. Who initiated things?

   c. What was my first impression?

   d. What exactly was it that attracted me at first?

   e. What was the best thing about the relationship?

   f. What were their most negative qualities (create a list)?

      (1) Once finished, read over all of your lists and circle any words or qualities that seem to repeat themselves from one person to another.

      (2) Make a "summary list" of those words or qualities that stand out.

(3) Take some time to think about your summary list and ask yourself the following questions?

    (a) Are there some patterns in my relationships of which I need to be aware?

    (b) Is there a trend I can see in my relationships over time? Getting healthier? Getting worse? Getting better and then a relapse?

    (d) Is my present partner significantly different from previous partners? Better? Worse? The same?

5. Recall someone who makes/made you feel great to be around and list three interior qualities of that person.

6. Concerning exterior qualities: Picture in your mind the one person that you feel is the ideal in looks. Which three features of theirs attract you the most?

7. Then: scan magazine covers, music compact disc covers and albums, video covers, and fashion magazines; examine people and list three examples of what pleasantly draws your attention to them as well as what does not. (Note not just physical traits, but expressions and activities as well.)

8. Analyze your fantasy turn-ons. In particular, the three you return to often. (Anything from a candlelight dinner to naughty and kinky can be listed here.)

Questions 1 and 2 were meant not only to awaken pleasant childhood memories of first crushes, but to reveal qualities in people that were distasteful to you even then. Questions 3 and 4 should have revealed to you: (1) The most painful relationship thus far in your life (longest list of negative qualities); (2) The healthiest and most satisfying relationship thus far in your life (shortest list of negative qualities); and (3) Whether your relationships are getting better or worse. Do the lists get shorter or do they get longer?

The answers to these questions should be revealing. Some patterns, both positive and negative, should be apparent. Once it's on paper, it's easy to see what kind of partners we've chosen in our lives. One of the most effective ways to sum up the kind of person you've been unknowingly seeking, whether in your past or today, is to create your own

Emotional Want Ad. Write an ad using the negative characteristics you have on your summary list; it's okay to make fun of yourself and your past choices.

Writing your Emotional Want Ad can be very powerful, because it forces you to look at the message you've been giving out about the kind of partner you are willing to accept. It's also a convincing way to break your own negative programming by taking what has been unconscious and making it conscious. The knowledge from this exercise should be empowering to you, because locating the persistent, negative patterns in your relationships is the first step toward eliminating them.

Questions 5 and 6 are to help you determine the physical traits and positive qualities you seek in a Dream Lover. They're meant to bring to mind everything that matters to you in looking for the right person. Good looks, sense of humor, honesty, professional career, religion and so on.

Take a tally. Rate on a scale from 1 to 10, how important each trait is to you in a partner. Once you've completed the assessment, using the same numbering system, rate *yourself* on each item. That will give you a clue as to whether you're being realistic and point out areas where you could use a little work.

People who exhibit the characteristics (face, figure, sex, activities, appearance, and personality) imprinted on our Love Map, are the ones we should choose to connect with to create the healthy, caring and loving relationships we desire.

Questions 7 and 8 are clues to what you find sensual and what turns you on. Knowing who you are and what you need and desire in a partner fosters the belief that "true love" is possible. The falling-in-love process of touching, laughing, and pleasuring, serves as the very essence of the feelings that stir inside of us when we're meeting someone we're attracted to for the first time. Our entire body seems to shout out, "Let's get it on!"

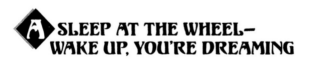 SLEEP AT THE WHEEL— WAKE UP, YOU'RE DREAMING

Not to confuse Dream Lover with sweet dreams, let's explore the meaning of some of your dreams. During the day, a rose is a rose, but in dreams that same rose probably symbolizes a thorn in your side. To understand your dreams—and his—you must first decode them. Some common dream symbols, and what they're saying about your relationship follow:

Chasing butterflies in a sunny meadow: You're happy, you're in love and you find your life interesting. Butterflies symbolize romance and happiness.

Tying an anchor around your lover's neck: You love him. Anchors represent strong attachment, devotion and loyalty.

Begging for an extra-large piece of cake: Your sex life could be better. Eating cake is seen as a sign wanting sexual fulfillment.

Making out with the milkman: Your relationship needs a bit of zest and some lightening up. Making love outside your relationship is a symbol of wishful thinking.

Eating an apple: You better stop flirting with that guy at the bus stop. Remember Adam and Eve? Apples are a warning of the dreadful consequences to your behavior.

Pouring water from a kettle: You aren't really happy in your relationship. A kettle means that you sense trouble brewing just around the corner.

Dream on, it's healthy and sometimes you'll wake up with solutions to some of your problems!

The Look of Love

In a recent *Esquire* poll, eyes ranked as the sexiest part of a man's body; general good looks ranked second. When one woman was asked the same question, without blinking she replied: "Oh, that's easy, I look at his eyes first. One look in a man's eyes and I know right away if I'm interested." When asked what kind of eyes turned her on, she then replied: "Oh, brown, I guess, or blue. It's not the color that matters, what's really important is what they *say* to me."

Eyes do not lie. They are the windows to the soul. They speak a language of their own and can tell a person's character in a moment. Love at first sight has survived because it is an integral part of immediate romantic love. The first peek of a potential lover often serves as the most powerful stimulus to kick-start a relationship.

A man may be classified as a breast man, a leg man or a buttocks man, and woman might be classified as a physique watcher or a butt watcher, but researchers have ascertained that *everybody* is an eye watcher. We have all used phrases like, "I fell in love the moment I looked into her eyes." "I love his baby blues." "She has sexy, bedroom eyes." "Wow, he undressed me with his eyes!" Eyes speak volumes and may well be the most revealing and accurate indicators of a person's true feelings.

People look lingeringly at sights they like and quickly turn away their eyes from things they don't like. We enjoy gazing for long, lazy hours into a cozy fire and feel calm while staring sleepily into the peacefulness of a setting sun. We gaze admiringly at our lovers, yet avoid the eyes of someone whom we feel might be unpleasant or dull.

Take 10 minutes to examine your eyes carefully. Find a mirror (preferably one that magnifies the image) and position a bright lamp to one side of you so that your eyes are fully illuminated. The light will cause your pupils to contract. Examine all the tiny details, and imprint the image on your mind. Then close your eyes, turn off the light and wait for 30 seconds. In the darkness your pupils will dilate. Then open your eyes and watch carefully how fast they have changed when you turn on the light again.

Study other people's eyes in real-life situations. Sit in a local restaurant or bar and observe what people do with their eyes. Notice how young couples in love spend minutes on end gazing deeply into each other's eyes. Watch how people flirt, "making eyes" at each other, or watch how someone waiting for a date glances nervously at his or her watch.

Notice whose eyes are scanning the room and whose eyes seem to pop out of their sockets in eager anticipation every time the bar door swings open. Watch how eyes flick down in disappointment when a stranger, rather than someone's longed-for partner, enters the room.

World experts agree that the larger our pupil size the more interested we are in what we are looking at, whether it's a movie, a magazine, or our lover; large pupils indicate interest and arousal.

Therefore, one of the completely uncontrollable sexual signals we all display is the dilation of our pupils. Setting a romantic mood by turning down the lights partly achieves its success through the consequent pupil dilation which makes us appear simultaneously attractive and more turned-on. It has exactly the same effect on our companion. That's why candlelight dinners are synonymous with romance. The luminous glow from a candle is not only flattering to skin color and texture, it encourages and shows off our pupil dilation.

CRUISING DOWN LOVER'S LANE

Poets and novelists have, for centuries, described coming under the spell of someone's looks, being bewitched and mesmerized by a single glance. People are capable of catching a potential lover with just their eyes and it happens in the most unexpected places.

The tiny exchange of glancing in a rear-view mirror and briefly meeting the reflected eyes of the driver behind, can make the heart beat faster and even cause the faint-hearted to feel as if they have been kicked in the chest by a mule. Seconds later, we go our different ways forever.

So many of us have regrets of missed opportunities. We fail to follow up the exchange of the initial spark, often glancing away without even returning an eyebrow flash, then the moment has passed and they're gone forever. Ever happened to you?

If someone starts an eye conversation with you and you like their look, then answer back. You have a lot to gain and little to lose.

C UPID'S ARROWS: SENSUAL PEEK-A-BOO

After the first burst of eye contact both parties naturally look away swiftly; this is part of the peek-a-boo phenomenon. The "now-you-see-me-now-you-don't" pleasure principle is one of the first games we learn as infants. It teaches us the excitement of anticipation. The longer the eyes are hidden, the greater the tension and the more pleasurable the relief when concealment is removed to reveal smiling eyes.

Understanding and applying the psychological effect of peek-a-boo in all areas of sexual communication is paramount to success in the secret world of nonverbal seduction. Adult peek-a-boo is seldom played with the hands, instead we use other objects to deliberately interrupt our eye-line. Actresses raise and lower fans provocatively to give a dramatic sensual effect. Brides lift their veil to reveal their face and eyes and women at masquerade balls raise and lower their hand-held masks in a teasing cat-and-mouse manner.

Sensual peek-a-boo is played out today without fancy props and costumes. People sitting at separate tables in a restaurant will lower a menu, a newspaper, a cup, a glass or even use other people to interrupt their line of vision to briefly admire or body scan another. If the glances are exchanged at least twice, a dance begins and there's a direct gaze for a couple of seconds.

If this eye-dance is to continue, mild smiles and slight head tilts follow. Up to this point, not a word has been spoken, but the two parties involved have participated in a delicious flirtation without obligation.

Done well, peek-a-boo is harmless, sensuous, and can be downright sexy. Long hair is wonderful for masking an eye, splits in skirts allow the wearer to tease admirers, rips in the seat of jeans enable the wearer to flash a tantalizing small surface of flesh and then hide it again simply by shifting position to close the gap in the material.

Once eyes meet again, scanning occurs. Scanning of your target lover's eyes a couple of times and then scanning their face, if sensitively done, is very pleasing. It is easy, though, to over-scan and stare. Seventy-five percent of a facial scan is devoted to exploring the eyes and mouth. A normal face scan lasts about three seconds, but, as with so many of the eye's sexual signals, a slight extension in duration to about four and a half seconds intensifies the emotional arousal of both parties.

F ULL BODY SCANS

Women and men tend to scan each other's bodies differently. Women who are flirting are far more subtle in the way they scan a man's full image. They spend much more time on his face (especially the mouth and eyes), his hair and overall size and build. Women also scan a man's clothes, particularly his shoes, as well as details like wedding rings and other jewelry or watches. For some women the length of a man's legs is also important, but not nearly as much of a visual turn-on, as the length of a woman's legs is for men.

I've created both a Man Well Worth Watching (MWWW) and a Woman Well Worth Watching (WWWW) organization. Members of the organization hand cards to men or women, informing the recipient that he or she is certified as someone "well worth watching" by the person handing the card. It's a way to check off what you like about someone else: their eyes, their smile, their walk, whatever.

It's an exciting and daring method to compliment someone else. Use and hand out the card on the following page (make as many copies of it as you need), to indicate to a person that they are "well worth watching." Have fun rewarding worthy people; after a time, everyone will want to be part of the group.

A good deal of a man's arousal is by visual stimulation, rather than by touch or tenderness. This explains why a guy can be all hot and bothered before a woman even feels a twinge of excitement. Women need to be stroked by gentle, caressing motions, whereas men have already been "stroked," from a simple vision of a woman in a great new dress or a sexy slip.

Men tend to be slightly more assertive and often offensive with their eyes. They are inclined to scan women from the ground up, feet first

You Are a Person Well Worth Watching

I'm attracted to your:
- ❏ Eyes
- ❏ Body
- ❏ Hair
- ❏ Good Looks
- ❏ Legs
- ❏ Smile
- ❏ Rear End
- ❏ Confidence
- ❏ Strength
- ❏ Humor
- ❏ Intelligence
- ❏ Personality

I'm _____

You can reach me at

_____

Thanks for letting me look!

and then legs, followed by crotch, torso, breasts, shoulders and face. The whole scan takes a second or less. If a woman feels that someone is staring too blatantly at her body, she will often automatically adjust her clothing to cover herself up. This is usually unpleasant for the woman and is unlikely to achieve positive results.

LOOKS MEN CAN'T RESIST

A man will make a decision about whether he finds you sexually irresistible within the first few seconds of setting eyes on you. Following are six looks to which men are especially responsive. Are you one of these or have you chosen your own version of the six looks to create your desirability?

Look Number 1:
The Waif

The key to this look is long, beautifully conditioned hair. It is slightly windblown if it's straight, and brushed out fully if it's curly. The hair has to be accompanied by darkly made-up, dreamy eyes and only the lightest of foundations. These looks seem to bring out a man's protective instincts.

The waif's lips are always slightly parted. She wears simple, short cotton dresses or oversized men's sweaters. She is always asking innocent questions that give men the opportunity to air their knowledge, but she doesn't pretend to be stupid. She has a way of asking for simple requests (unscrewing pickle jars, opening wine bottles, or fastening jewelry) that involve physical touching and an unexpected degree of intimacy. The waif's apparent innocence allows her to be quite "touchy" from the moment she meets a man. She holds hands, links arms and when she leaves, gives soft, trembly kisses to the men who attract her.

Look Number 2:
The Free Spirit

The free spirit wears soft, gauzy dresses that are temptingly see-through, or she wears caftans or billowy blouses with decorated jeans. She always wears lots of jingly silver and enamel bracelets and is very friendly and calm. Her make-up concentrates on her eyes and she uses an unusual cheek blusher to give more definition to her face. She gives men the impression that she is at peace with herself and that she's very giving and shares easily.

She has taught herself to read palms (a wonderful way to flirt, involving holding hands, touching, tickling, as well as a way to say flattering things to a man she hardly knows).

The free spirit listens to men carefully and tells them they obviously have great character and sensitivity. Men are attracted to her because they feel she's sensual but independent, and that she conveys a sense of mystery, which they find provocative. To the men she finds attractive, the free spirit gives a small good luck gift when she leaves, and tells them that a gift always finds its way of returning to the giver. Thus, her method of letting him know that she expects to see him again.

Look Number 3:
The Country-and-
Western Gal

Many men find the Country-and-Western look irresistible. You need bouncy bobbed hair and natural make-up to give you that fresh "Oh what a beautiful morning" appearance. Go for skintight denim jeans and checkered shirts with the first three buttons undone and the collar turned up in an authentic Doris Day style.

A Stetson isn't necessary, but don't forget your big shiny belt buckle and your little high-heeled boots. Men are attracted to the Country-and-Western woman's independence, strength and personal freedom.

She usually tells a man she likes the outdoors and that there's nothing more romantic than looking up on a summer's night and counting the stars. Men ask for their loving advice because of the Country-and-Western woman's knowledge of those emotional simple-hearted songs about heartbreak and tears.

Look Number 4:
The Secretarial Look

Men have the romantic notion in their heads that every woman with a French twist, glasses and a severe suit, is underneath a seething volcano of suppressed lust. "Why, Ms. Robinson, without your glasses, you're . . . you're beautiful!"

This look appeals to men who like a challenge, and like to believe that they have unparalleled powers of seduction. The idea of you taking off your glasses and letting your hair down gives them a sense of sexual power, especially if they think that you're wearing a black garter belt and black stockings underneath your sensible skirt.

There's a trick to the secretarial look. It doesn't work if you simply put on any old pair of glasses; work with frames that are best for you. It's extraordinary how a good pair of glasses can flatter your features— emphasizing your cheekbones or lightening a heavy jaw.

The secretarial look calls for more makeup than the other looks. Shades of startling scarlet lipstick, well-fitted suits, discreet jewelry and immaculate nails work best to capture the true secretarial look.

She's a good listener and usually laughs at a man's jokes, but she also talks about the things she likes. During conversations that particularly interest or excite her, she briefly takes off her glasses, gives her partner a sparkly-eyed look, and then puts her glasses back on again.

The secretarial woman has at her disposal one of the greatest flirtation techniques ever—the speck in the eye. She pretends to have something in her eye and asks for help in taking it out. After taking her glasses off, the man usually has to stand close to her, while she holds on to his arm to steady herself. It's one of the most intimate things you can ask of a stranger.

Another is to ask for assistance while cleaning your glasses. The reflection-free glasses that are so popular, can only be cleaned using material made from 100 percent cotton. In one of my flirting episodes, I asked a gentleman, "If he had anything 100 percent cotton on himself that I could use to clean my spectacles?" It brought about much laughter. He thought I was referring to his underwear, when I was really referring to his hanky!!

Look Number 5:
The Exotic

Many men are very strongly aroused by the idea of dating a woman who's nationality is different. The unknown is intriguing, appealing and charming.

Your own exotic look will depend on your facial features, your complexion and possibly your ethnic origin. If you have any ethnic features or ethnic background, use them to your advantage to give yourself a distinctive look of your own. Your hair, your eyes, your voice, the way you smile, and your individual ethnic beauty is what makes him melt.

Emphasizing your own personal ethnic looks can make you feel more yourself, more relaxed and more fun. It boosts your self-confidence and does wonders for your luck with men. The point is to make the most of your own individual appearance, and to make yourself look interesting, attractive and different.

Look Number 6:
The Voluptuous One

It's a strange paradox. Although so many women are constantly diet-ing, the truth is that men like curvy, voluptuous women. If you have a fuller figure, exploit it. You have only one life and one body and if you're not going to be proud of yourself now, then when? Understand that you are just as sexy as the next woman, and that there are plenty of men out there who love you just the way you are.

Wear clothes that show your confidence in yourself. For the full-figured woman, the key to looking sexy is to look smart. Take extra care with your hair, emphasize your good points, and pay particular attention to your eyes and your lips. If you have big breasts, flaunt them.

When it comes to finding yourself a man, don't make your size a pri-ority. Dress well, act normal, eat a regular balanced diet and stay calm. Your provocative, but businesslike, attractiveness will shine.

SUMMARY

When considering the look that might work best for you, remember that it's important not to try to be somebody you're not. Be realistic about your age and your physical appearance.

Making yourself appealing has to do with enhancing yourself, not hiding yourself. When you walk into that room and see that man you fancy, he won't be looking at your flaws; he'll be looking at a woman who smiles, a woman who feels good about herself and a woman who shows that she's genuinely interested in what he is and what he does.

THE EYEBROW FLASH

When spotting someone across a room who we find attractive, we respond automatically with an eyebrow flash when they look our way. It lasts about a fifth of a second and is duplicated in every culture on earth.

The eyebrow flash is only employed when we wish to acknowledge another person's presence, as it is a messenger to an exchange. Raising them or raising and lowering them is a universal sign that the human animal has seen something interesting. Raised eyebrows also indicate an attitude that is receptive and open to an advance. Returning an eyebrow flash is one of the top flirting gestures exhibited by women and sends a clear message for further communication.

STARING, GAZING, WINKING

Staring and gazing are not at all the same thing: one is attacking and the other is inviting. A stare is like shooting invisible arrows from your eyes into the eyes of the person on the receiving end, leaving them cold and defensive or feeling invaded.

The contrast between staring and gazing is dramatic. When we gaze, our whole face is softer and our eyes appear gentle. People in love spend ages gazing into each other's eyes. It is almost as though they are unconsciously reaching for the deeper, intuitive secrets of their lover.

Women generally find gazing much simpler than men do. When men try the same thing, they usually blow it because they stare. Women who gaze well (using deep, dreamy, hypnotic glances) can make a man's toes curl or his heart flush in a second.

Winking is a fantastically powerful sexual signal. It can signify a shared secret, something special or a flirtatious invitation. Men are more successful using winks that are subtle and delicate. The "quieter" the wink from a man, the more devastating it is to receive. When it is delivered with a gentle smile, it almost can't be resisted.

A sly wink from a woman can also have a sensational effect upon a man. Long eyelashes, which enhance the apparent size of the eye, provide a dramatic effect and act like a pair of wide-open arms irresistibly inviting someone to come near.

Speaking of long lashes, one of the most erotic ways to touch someone early in an intimate encounter is to give them "butterfly kisses." This is accomplished when you gently caress the cheek and maybe the nose of the other person with the tips of the eyelashes of one eye. Try it now on the palm of your hand if you've never tried it before. Feels good, doesn't it? Does it tickle? Try it on someone soon and let them feel the immense sexual charm of your eyes and your eyelashes.

LINGERING LOOKS

During normal conversations, people tend to look briefly away at the end of a sentence or during silences, *except* when they are engrossed in the listener (or hopelessly in love). The phrase, "he couldn't take his eyes off her," proves that people who are in love are more hesitant to take their eyes off each other, even after they have finished speaking. It is almost electrifying when someone's glance lingers on you during silence after you've stopped talking.

Next time you're talking with someone who interests you, let your eyes stay glued to his or hers a little longer—even during the silences. It is almost unnerving and when you must look away, do so reluctantly. Drag your eyes away slowly, as though they had been stuck with warm taffy.

A prominent Harvard psychologist, Zick Rubin, became fascinated with how to measure love by recording the time lovers spent staring into each other's eyes. It had been determined that people, when talking, look at one another only 30 to 60 percent of the time. That's not long enough to rev up the engines of love at first sight.

Rubin found that people who were deeply in love gaze at each other 75 percent of the time when talking and are slower to look away when somebody intrudes in their world. This young romantic researcher produced the first psychometrically-based scale to determine how much affection couples felt for each other. It's known as *Rubin's Scale* and, to this day, many social psychologists use it to determine people's feelings.

Extra seconds of eye contact speak volumes in the look of love—they're considered naughty, but nice.

WANTED: SEXY BEDROOM EYES AT HOTEL CALIFORNIA

Marilyn Monroe, Paul Newman, Sharon Stone, and Clark Gable do not have the patent on bedroom eyes. It is not a quality movie stars are blessed with, but it is a quality that can be developed. It's a quality that we all possess, and one that is buried deep in our seductive talents. Researchers call this look, the copulatory gaze. And, yes, it does play a big role in lovemaking.

What makes our eyes sexy and inviting? Quite simply, large pupils. Large pupils are more alluring and more stimulating than small pupils. When we look at an enticing stimulus, our pupils expand. If you are truly interested or intrigued by a movie, a book or a picture, your pupils do dilate.

To create this look on your own, try this. While you're with someone that you find attractive and the two of you are chatting, simply gaze at the most attractive feature on his face. Does he have adorable dimples? Does he have inviting lips? As your eyes enjoy the sight, your pupils will gradually expand, giving you those bedroom eyes.

Also, think loving thoughts. Concentrate on how beautiful your lover is, how comfortable you feel with him, and how much fun it would be to shower with him. Boy, if that doesn't make your eyes larger, nothing will.

Ever watch a guy's eyes while he thumbs through *Playboy* magazine? *Men's Health* magazine has proven that, "A good deal of men's arousal is by visual stimulation, rather than by touch or tenderness." To be aroused, women feel the need to be stroked and held. Men, on the other hand, can feel excitement simply by a vision. Be it that of his lover in a great new dress or a sexy slip, he's way ahead of her on the arousal curve. Never underestimate the power of images; looks kill!

"Women in New York City wear a lot of black stockings and high heels with their career clothes," says a Wall Street broker. "They've got to be the sexiest women in the world. I don't know how they do it, but they look smart, powerful, *and sexy.*"

EMOTIONS OF THE FACE

Next to the eyes, the face is the most powerful means by which we communicate nonverbally. We use it, and others rely on it, to express our emotional state at the moment and to indicate how attentive we are to their feelings. Humans have three profound needs: appreciation, attention, and affection. Attending to these needs in yourself and in others will bring more love to your life.

Messages about loving are sent to others from our hearts as well as our bodies. Appreciation means genuinely showing others that you treasure them. Attention is the ability to listen with the totality of your being. And, affection means showing someone in an open, loving way that you care for them.

Just as the sun is always shining, the heart is always open and the face is constantly telling others of our awareness and our aliveness. Once eye contact with another leads to a smile, a kind of psychological visibility has been established.

> *"None of us has the power to make someone else love us. But we all have the power to give away love, to love other people. And if we do, we change the kind of person we are, they are, and we change the kind of world we live in."*
>
> by *Rabbi Harold Kushner*

Acknowledging another through our facial expressions at least keeps them aware that we've recognized them. Our facial expressions reveal certain aspects of our personality, our attitudes toward others, our sexual attraction and attractiveness, our desire to communicate or initiate interaction and even our state of health.

The face is the language of emotions. Different parts of it are used to display different emotions. Fear is usually looked for in the eyes, as is sadness. Happiness is seen in the cheeks and the mouth as well as in the eyes. Surprise is seen in the forehead, eyes and mouth. Anger is usually expressed throughout the face. Be aware that women display facial emotions more easily and more readily than men do, therefore, they're easier to read.

A woman needs to feel emotionally close to make love. A man needs to make love to feel emotionally close. So, maybe you aren't from Mars and your lover isn't from Venus, despite what those books say. Maybe the two of you are from Pluto and Saturn. Or Houston or Hollywood. Or First Street and Second Avenue. The fact is that men and women are different in crucial emotional ways. Women want warmth and sincerity. Men want affection. *Vive la différence!*

Mona Lisa, Marilyn or Madonna's smile

Smiles, normally used as a greeting gesture, generally indicate varying degrees of pleasure, amusement and happiness. In some contexts, though, they can show aggression and sarcasm.

Considering the difference between Mona Lisa's partial smile and Marilyn Monroe's poutingly, coy mouth, we realize there exists a great variety of smiles. Let's examine the following:

The closed-mouth smile	is used when we are smiling to ourselves.
The tight-lipped smile	indicates suppressed anger or pain.
The full or broad smile	is symmetrical, and laughter lines appear on the face and around the eyes.
The false smile	is indicated by the tight jaw and top lid, narrowed eyes and lack of laughter lines.
The hostile smile	is an exaggerated full-teeth smile.

The genuine, happy smile	lights up the whole face. The eyes sparkle, the cheekbones lift, the smiling lines around the eyes and mouth are obvious and the jaw muscles are relaxed.
The sexual smile	is coy, with either pouty lips or a slight bite on one side of the lower lip.

Both men and women (but more so women) tend to bare their teeth as they become aroused. Your smile will be one of your most attractive assets; people are automatically attracted to smiling faces. The ability to make others smile and laugh is sexy. After a good laugh, our bodies are in a state of arousal very similar to when we are sexually turned on: we breathe in and out very deeply and our blood circulation is heightened, causing the surface of the skin to blush.

Anxious or miserable expressions are so unsexy. A glowing natural smile has a potent effect: it makes us feel better emotionally, more relaxed, more confident, more optimistic and even more hopeful. It allows the recipient of our smile to feel good inside too. It is as infectious as it is attractive, and combined with good eye contact, it packs a punch and strongly sends a positive message.

Y OU'VE GOT THE LOOK

It's easy to spot people who have fallen in love. They stand taller, walk a little faster and seem to smile a lot more often. Therefore, it probably won't surprise most people to learn that studies into the mind/body connection confirm that being in love has a positive effect on a person's health.

Being in love puts a smile on your face, and experts estimate that 100 hardy laughs yield the same aerobic benefit as 15 minutes on a stationary bike. More importantly, intimacy boosts the immune system by busting stress. Self-disclosure within a close relationship produces a calming effect by relaxing the muscles and providing a buffer zone during times of stress. Help your heart; fall in love!!

YOU LOOK SO GOOD IN LOVE

Just how romantic are you and what is your love style? Is it Eros, Ludus, or Storge? Woooooo, what do these mean? We'll find out in a minute. Answer how strongly you agree or disagree with each following statement as it relates to your current relationship. If you aren't in a relationship right now, think of your ideal relationship and your beliefs about relationships in general. To complete the test, indicate the extent to which you agree with each item using the scale below:

> 5 = strongly agree
> 4 = agree
> 3 = sometimes
> 2 = disagree
> 1 = strongly disagree

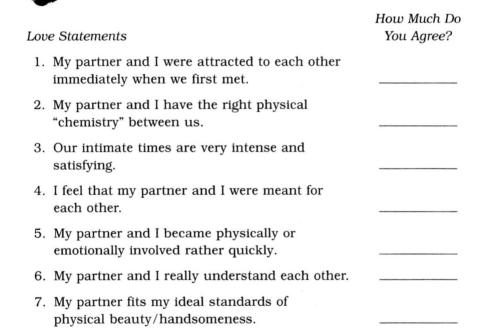

	How Much Do
Love Statements	*You Agree?*

1. My partner and I were attracted to each other immediately when we first met. _____

2. My partner and I have the right physical "chemistry" between us. _____

3. Our intimate times are very intense and satisfying. _____

4. I feel that my partner and I were meant for each other. _____

5. My partner and I became physically or emotionally involved rather quickly. _____

6. My partner and I really understand each other. _____

7. My partner fits my ideal standards of physical beauty/handsomeness. _____

Eros Subscore _____

8. I try to keep my partner a little uncertain about my commitment to him/her. _____

9. I believe that what my partner doesn't know
    about me won't hurt him/her.   _____

10. I have sometimes had to keep two of my
    partners from finding out about each other.   _____

11. I can get over love affairs pretty easily and
    quickly.   _____

12. My partner would get upset if she/he knew
    of some of the things I've done with other people.   _____

13. When my partner gets too dependent on me,
    I want to back off a little.   _____

14. I enjoy playing the "game of love" with a
    number of different partners.   _____

    Ludus Subscore   _____

15. It is hard to say exactly where the friendship
    ends and love begins.   _____

16. I cannot love unless I've first had caring for
    a while.   _____

17. I still have good friendships with almost
    everyone with whom I have ever been involved
    in a love relationship.   _____

18. The best kind of love grows out of a long
    friendship.   _____

19. It is hard to say exactly when my partner and
    I fell in love.   _____

20. Love is really a deep friendship, not a
    mysterious, mystical emotion.   _____

21. My most satisfying love relationships have
    developed from good friendships.   _____

    Storge Subscore   _____

SCORING AND EVALUATION

For each of the subsections, add up the total and enter it below. The
subsection scores are associated with three main love styles that are
related to how you feel:

1. Eros (passionate) score: _____

2. Ludus (playful) score: _____

3. Storge (friendship) score: _____

The range for each subscore is from 7 to 35. Identify your love style by finding the highest score. These categories give you a sense of the kind of lover you tend to be—even if you aren't in a relationship right now. If you are in a relationship, the questions can help describe what you are like in that relationship. Consider asking your partner to take this test, too, and then see how well you match.

What do these categories mean? These terms are derived from three Greek words for different kinds of love:

Eros: stands for passionate love. People who are currently in love are particularly likely to be identified with Eros. Eros involves strong physical preferences and responses to a lover, and a lot of commitment.

Ludus: stands for game-playing love. People who score high in this category approach love as an interactional game— even if it sometimes involves deception. Ludus types may even be wary of closeness. People who have never been in love and those who have been in love again and again and again tend to fit well into this category. People who have been in love only once or twice are not as likely to belong in this category.

Storge: those who scored high in storge have an inclination to link love and friendship. It is an enduring kind of love, but it is not a particularly passionate kind of love.

If you take this test with your partner, matching is ideal. If you and your partner's scores for each "love type" are less than 6 points apart, you should consider that as a very good match. More than 10 points difference between the two of you, indicates a huge difference in what each of you feels is solid romantic love.

3 The Closer I Get to You

Dear Diary:

My body shakes in his presence. Screaming with every glance. Alarms of attraction go off: emotional, physical, spiritual, sexual, intellectual. Should I run before it's too late? No way. I feel an addiction coming on.

While boarding a plane to visit a potential lover, I saw him. Confident and intense, just the way I like'm. Feeling like a cat, I became curious. Stalking him, I moved in. My whiskers ruffled. What a rare find. He's coming my way. Electricity danced in the air. Closer. Closer. Caught! Shucks, he caught me looking, but he looked too.

Purring began as our conversation approached intimacy. I'm late for my plane, he is too. We went our separate ways. Him for a vacation. Me to another man. I look back, WOW, he's looking back too, and smiling. So dramatic. So much fun. So sexy. I hope he calls. Pleeeeeeease, please, let him call!

Tallulah Bankhead once said, "It's the good girls who keep the diaries; the bad girls never have the time." We're too busy smiling, talking, playing, dancing, laughing and flirting; that's why I threw mine away years ago.

Romance is thought to be made in heaven, but seduction and arousal can happen any time a possible lover gets close to you. It's a combination of candlelight, flowers, music, dinners, boat rides, dancing, courting, complimenting, confiding and caring. Many think that the responsibility for "the return to romance," rests on the man's shoulders.

Surprisingly enough, though, research proves that women initiate 85 percent of all flirtatious encounters. Furthermore, when these flirtatious encounters are initiated, they are returned by the intended male.

When you examine the list of "Who's Who of Great Flirts," you'll notice how women outnumber men.

Mae West	Brigitte Bardot
Eva Peron	Coco Chanel
Marilyn Monroe	Madonna
Snow White and two of the Dwarfs	Sharon Stone
Catherine the Great	Scarlett O'Hara
Daisy Mae	Lucille Ball
Ellie Mae	Juliet
Any Miss Congeniality	Miss Piggy
Joan Collins	Cleopatra
Minnie Mouse	Barbie
Lois Lane	Pocahontas
Picasso	Casanova
Henry VIII	Clark Gable

No matter what you think, to be a great flirt it's not necessary to be devastatingly attractive, rich, smooth or good at batting your eyelashes. These assets are just window dressing for the successful flirt. Learning how to fascinate, titillate, captivate and be great at love's most amusing sport, gives you the advantage in the mating game.

OBSERVE SPEED LIMITS DURING THE ATTENTION-GETTING PHASE

American singles-bar courtship has several stages, each with distinctive escalation points. The first is the "attention-getting" phase. Men and women do this somewhat differently. As soon as they enter the bar, both males and females typically establish a territory. It's either a seat, a place to lean, or a position somewhere on the dance floor. Once they're settled, they begin to attract attention to themselves.

Tactics vary. Men tend to roll their shoulders, stretch, stand tall, and shift from foot to foot in a swaying motion. They also exaggerate their body movements. Instead of simply using the wrist to stir a drink, men often employ the entire arm. Even the normally smooth motion necessary to light a cigarette becomes a whole-body gesture, ending with an elaborate shaking from the elbow to extinguish the match. Also, the whole body is employed in hearty laughter, sometimes loud enough to attract a crowd.

"It is better to be looked over, than overlooked," Mae West once said, and women know it. Women begin the attention-getting phase with many of the same maneuvers that men use, often incorporating a battery of feminine moves as well. They twist their curls, tilt their heads, look up coyly, giggle, lick their upper lips, raise their brows, blush and hide their faces in order to signal, "I am here."

Some women also have a characteristic walk when courting; they arch their backs, thrust out their bosoms, sway their hips, and strut. No wonder women wear high-heeled shoes. This Western custom, invented by Catherine de Medici in the 1500s, unnaturally arches the back, tilts the buttocks, and thrusts the chest out into a female come-hither pose.

With a high-heeled gait, puckered lips, batting eyes, dancing brows, rocking bodies and swaying skirts, women signal approachability similar to that of a green light.

INTREPRETING THE DISTANCE AND THE BLIND SPOT

The "recognition" stage starts once the eyes have met. You can tell if someone is attracted to you by interpreting the distance between the two of you. Before we get started with this interpretation, let's mentally distinguish three crucial markers.

20 feet or more away	"Screening Line"
5–6 feet away	"Attraction Line"
You	"Finish Line"

THE SCREENING LINE

The screening line is usually the point in which someone will notice you; it's perhaps 25 feet or so from you. When you get a look from a man at this distance, it is nothing to be excited about. This is the first time a man sees you, so he's looking to see what you look like. It will take him 30 seconds to process whether you are his type or not (it takes women three seconds to size someone up and know whether she is interested or not). If he likes what he sees, he will want to see you at a closer range. If this is the case, he will hold his stare for any amount of time. Men feel safe staring when they are this far away from you because the distance is not an intimate range.

THE ATTRACTION LINE

The attraction line has important meaning. This is the line in which men decide whether they want to meet you. In the screening line, they were checking you out, now they are five to six feet away, and they already know they find you attractive. If a man does not like you, it is very easy to tell. He simply won't look at you again, and he will continue past the finish line and lose the race.

The attraction line represents the time he is thinking of ways to meet you. The man is formulating his plan and may even begin to turn the opposite direction to where you are while figuring out a way to meet you without making a fool of himself. He is almost guaranteed to come back your way once he has a couple of minutes to plan.

For men who don't see you at the screening line, the chances of meeting are less because they haven't been allowed the processing time to see whether you are their type. If a man sees you for the first time, and he's already at the attraction line area, if he likes you, he will look at you in a certain way. First, he will give you a "stranger glance" (a glance that lasts only one to two seconds), just because he notices a woman in his field of vision. Then he will immediately look at you again. If a man looks at you a third time, shout hooray! He likes you. The third look is a charm; he wants to meet you. He then goes into the behaviors mentioned earlier that signal his attraction to you.

THE FINISH LINE

Regardless of attraction, if a man first notices you at the finish line, then your chance of meeting him is almost zero. It's almost too late. Rarely will a man who first notices you at this close range, turn back around and come your way. Once that man passes, start looking at the screening line for another man. The finish line is just that; a place to mark the end of a race.

Your chances of a man liking you are improved if he sees you at the screening line first, looks again at the attraction line, and avoids crossing the finish line. As mentioned, if he looks at you a third time, you've got it made. He's interested! Some men, though, are afraid of rejection, and will not take the initiative to meet a woman even if they are interested. They feel they need a "reason" to approach women. Therefore, if you're interested in an approaching man, comment on something he has with him or something he's wearing. Try to make it a little easier for him. Remember, it's a chance you need to take to find a partner.

IMITATION: THE SINCEREST FLATTERY

What we like, we copy. If we fall in love, we copy on the deepest level possible. As sexual interest develops, we begin to imitate our potential partner's way of behaving. By mirroring movements and matching his or her rhythms with our own, we send strong signals of sexual interest.

Body synchrony is the most intriguing component of the pickup. It is accomplished when one person takes up a particular body posture and the other follows them, moving to adopt a similar or even identical posture between five and 50 seconds later. As potential lovers become comfortable, they pivot or swirl until their shoulders become aligned, their bodies face-to-face. This rotation toward each other and synchrony start even before they begin to talk. When he lifts his drink, she lifts hers. When he crosses his legs, she crosses hers; as he leans left, she leans left; when he smoothes his hair, she smoothes hers.

This knowledge can be used to move closer to a potential partner. Slowly, subtly, without mimicking and with respect, we can take up the nonverbal movements of someone that sparks our interest and hope the signals are returned. The more someone follows your movements, the more interested he is in you. The real art, though, is to echo the other person's posture without copying them exactly.

Human mirroring begins in infancy. We copied the way our parents walked, talked, played and worked. As we grew, we mirrored those people whom we admired, whose way of moving through the world seemed to us worth having. If we are in love, then it is our partner whom we admire and copy. We begin a sexual dance and establish a beat, or rhythm once we feel comfortable with our new admirer.

To dance is natural, therefore, it is reasonable to suggest that as we become attracted to each other, we begin to keep a common beat. Couples who reach total body synchrony will, at cocktail parties, church socials, office luncheons or other informal settings, sit alike, stand alike and often leave together. As Shakespeare elegantly said, "If music be the food of love, play on."

FIFTEEN BODY LANGUAGE SIGNS THAT SHOW HIS INTEREST

1. He will lean forward.

2. The front of his body will face you directly.

3. He will tilt his head.

4. He will sit on the edge of his chair to get closer to you.

5. He will touch his face often, especially as he looks at you.

6. He will smile either at you or to himself when you are around. This is an unconscious way for him to look appealing and draw attention to himself.

7. He will display grooming behaviors (slick his hair down, straighten his tie, check his teeth).

8. He will exaggerate body movements to get you to notice him.

9. He will moisten his lips.

10. He will play with his clothes; predominantly, he will pull up his socks.

11. He will touch you briefly, accidentally or on purpose.

12. He will laugh or clear his throat to get your attention.

13. He will look at your mouth, not just your eyes, when he talks to you. Men have admitted that they look at a woman's mouth and imagine kissing her.

14. If he crosses his leg, it will be in your direction.

15. He will sit or stand within six feet of where you are. This makes him close enough to say something to you.

These body signs are subconscious; they work as an automatic reflex in response to attraction. When someone is attracted to another, there is a natural urge to get as close to that person as possible. One man put it this way: "When I like a woman, all I want to do is to get as close to her as I can, to smell her hair, her perfume, to lightly brush her hand. It feels like a driving force behind my conscious thoughts." Groucho Marx, concerning the subject of romance, put it another way when he said, "If I hold you any closer, I'll be in back of you."

FIFTEEN BODY LANGUAGE SIGNS THAT SHOW HER INTEREST

1. She will smile broadly at you.
2. She will throw you a short, darting glance.
3. She'll dance alone to the music or snap her fingers in an effort to keep time to the beat of the music.
4. She will look straight at you and flip her hair.
5. She will look at you, toss her head, then look back at you.
6. She will cross and uncross her legs in slow calculated movements.
7. She will finally cross her upper leg toward you and keep it there.
8. She will begin to thrust (kick) her crossed leg up and down.
9. She will dangle her shoe.
10. She then will tilt her head slightly and touch her exposed neck.
11. She will casually expose her wrist.
12. She will lick her lips during eye contact.
13. She will primp while keeping eye contact.
14. While walking, she will used exaggerated hip movement.
15. If close enough, she will accidentally brush up against you.

Women should not hesitate to make the first move. Don't feel he'll think you are too forward if you smile broadly at him in a crowd or accidentally brush up against him. He won't, because, happily, the male ego takes over and ten minutes later, he won't even realize that he was not the one who made the initial approach.

INVADING SPACE WITH OBJECTS

People often use objects to invade another person's space. Pens, wine glasses, cigarettes or candles can be slid across table tops as if they were chess pieces being sent as ambassadors on a mission to represent our heart's desire.

While enjoying a romantic, candlelight dinner try sliding a pen, lighter or glass over the halfway mark of the table into the other person's space, their reaction will be telling. If your partner takes hold of the object and strokes it, or keeps touching it, then they're attracted to you. If they push the object back onto your side of the table, you should back off and accept the fact that romance may not be in the air, or at least take a clear hint that you are rushing things and your partner wants you to slow down.

Every action, once someone has entered your intimate space zone, suggests unconscious feelings. Even the provocative fondling of a wine glass stem by a man or a woman in close proximity to you speaks sexual volumes.

Sometimes we leave objects behind in people's personal space "accidentally on purpose": a pair of glasses, a pen, an umbrella, a precious piece of clothing; these are all ways of saying that we do not want to leave, and are providing a good excuse for returning another day. This may even happen without our being consciously aware of it.

INVADING SPACE WITH OUR BODIES

People invade the personal space of others with various parts of their bodies. Our hands are our most obvious nonverbal communicators. Hands make gestures to represent actual words, symbolize acts, and illustrate, emphasize and enliven our verbal conversations. We also often have ample opportunity to place our hands where they can be touched by another person.

From the formal non-threatening handshake to the intimate stroke of the neck or face, the hands are used to indicate interest in another person. The manner in which our hands are employed will indicate the intent that lies behind the gesture. We use our arms and legs, too, in the personal space dance of love. When we are attracted to someone we will often point at them, not obviously, with a finger, but quietly and seductively, with our hands and arms, our legs, feet and toes. It is as if we want to unconsciously indicate our sexual interest in someone by pointing at them, to select them from a crowd.

We point with our hands at our own best sexual assets, and also at the parts of our body, we might like caressed the most. Being alert to body pointing empowers you to analyze what is happening between two people.

TAILGATING AND OTHER FORMS OF SPACE INVASION

Two people can be arm in arm in their minds even when they are standing 50 feet apart. This can be witnessed on a dance floor, where strangers at opposite ends of the room may move in perfect synchrony as if they were adjacent to each other, or when someone hugs themselves as if to say, "This is you in my arms."

We can take people into our intimate space in our imaginations and can indicate intense desire with gestures. For example, we cup our hands over our heart as if to say, "I love you," or we blow someone a kiss to say "goodbye."

We also use inanimate objects to represent ourselves in other people's space. We give mementos, letters, flowers and gifts, all of which are symbolic of our actual selves. If a woman knows her letter is pinned to her target lover's bedroom wall, then part of her is there with him. That's why clothes are so intimate; when a man lends a woman his jacket and she wraps it around her shoulders, it is as though she is being protected by him. The same is true of the old trick of catching a man's attention by dropping a handkerchief or glove. It's done with the intention of creating an excuse for making his acquaintance.

NO PASSING: BARRICADES AND BODY BLOCKS

Body blocks are twofold. First, blocking can be a way to establish boundaries around you and the person whom you are attempting to seduce. It is a manner by which you create a private and safe haven for your partner.

We use our bodies as shields to mark out our territory from rivals, particularly at parties. A common mistake, made especially by men, is to block a woman into a corner or up against a bar so as to stifle her or make her feel trapped. Established lovers do this obviously with their arms interlocking as they face each other or simply by sending a message of, "Is there anyone else in this room but us?" to others as they longingly gaze at each other.

Second, blocking is also a useful skill for sending, "I'm not interested" messages without having the embarrassment of needing to spell it out in words. By building a wall of nonverbal blocks around us, we can protect ourselves, comfort ourselves and warn others off. Our arms, legs, shoulders and body positions can all be employed as means of saying, "No thanks."

The most common body block that is displayed as a sign of non-interest, is that of folding one or both arms across the chest. In essence, a barrier is formed in an attempt to block out undesirable circumstances. Many people claim that they habitually take the arms-folded position because it is comfortable. But one thing is certain: when a person experiences a nervous, negative or defensive attitude, he will fold his arms firmly on his chest indicating a strong signal that he feels threatened.

There are many arm-folding positions of disinterest. We will examine the three most common ones. Seeing the standard arm-cross gesture (arms crossed over chest with only one set of fingers exposed), reasonably assures you that you may have said something with which the other person disagrees. Therefore, it may be pointless to continue your line of argument even though the other person may be verbally agreeing with you. Nonverbal gestures do not lie; mouths lie. A simple, but effective, method of breaking the folded-arms position is to hand the cross-armed person a pen, a drink, a book or something that forces him to unfold his arms and reach forward. This move allows him to take a more open, receptive posture.

The second body block is the reinforced arm-crossed position. In this position, the arms are again crossed over the chest, but this time the fists are tightly clenched and are beneath each arm. The person using this cluster of gestures displays a hostile and defensive attitude. This type of arm cross is often combined with clenched teeth, a red face and an attacking attitude.

The third body block requires that the hands tightly grip the upper arms, after the arms have been crossed over the chest. This pose is taken by those who want to reinforce the blocking position and to stop any attempt to unfold the arms and expose the body. The arms, in this case, can often be gripped so tightly that the fingers and knuckles turn white as blood circulation is cut off. This serious blocking position shows an extremely negative restrained attitude.

The full-arm cross gesture is sometimes too obvious to use around others, therefore, we substitute a more discreet version. Some of the more discerning body-block positions we see are:

1. The partial arm-cross; in which only one arm swings across the body to hold or touch the other arm.

2. Holding hands with oneself; where the hands meet in front of the body, down over the genital area. (Desmond Morris states that this gesture allows a person to relive the emotional security he experienced as a child when his parent held his hand during fearful circumstances.)

3. Disguised arm-crossed gestures; where one arms swings across in front of the body to grasp the other arm, but instead of arms folding, one hand touches a bracelet, watch, shirt cuff, button, cuff link or other object on or near the other arm.

4. Women are less obvious than men in their use of disguised arm-barrier gestures, because they can place books, notebooks or purses across their chests when they become unsure of themselves. Women will use a glass of beer or wine or even use a bouquet of flowers, held with two hands, to form an almost undetectable arm barrier.

DOES "NO" EVER MEAN "YES?"

Men have wondered for years, "What the heck do I say when she asks, 'Do you think it looks like I've gained weight?'"

Women are experts at posing questions that seem to have no right answer and there is no answer to this question that won't be interpreted "yes." "No" means yes. "Yes" means yes. "I don't know" means yes. "It doesn't matter" means yes. The briefest hint of a pause before speaking means, yes, yes, yes! Most men would rather take the SATs again than field this one, yet it may come up several times a week.

To be careful, probably their only safe choice is to say "no," clearly and immediately, leaving no possibility for any subtext, and making it sound like it's a widely acknowledged fact and not simply their opinion. This doesn't actually work either, but all the other opinions are worse.

Now that I think of it though, men also have been known to ask their mates similar questions. Perhaps something like, "Have you started to notice my double chin?" What's a girl to do?

What men and women are actually wanting, when asking questions like these, is for their mates to lend them just that smattering of assurance they need to ease their minds that they're still attractive and that they look okay. True, he or she won't entirely believe you when the answer is "no," but at least they'll be thinking that you respect them enough to give them the first straight answer that comes to your mind.

That's why it's so important that your partner just says "no." Respecting our partners, and their right to constantly ask such tricky, frustrating questions is fundamental to the encouragement and support needed in any relationship. We all need reassurance and approval, but from our mates it is truly essential to our well-being.

While dating and when in love, "no" can sometimes mean "yes." Possibly the flirting pull-back really means "come and get me." Sometimes though, "no" really does mean "no," whether the person has the courage to say it straight out, or has to signal it in more discreet ways. So, how do we tell?

People who tell us "no" with clear eye contact, with a straight and square body position and with an even, balanced voice tone, have to be taken seriously. They mean it. And, if we want others to know that we mean it too, we can adopt this body talk when we face someone and have to tell them a genuine "no." All too often, however, such a clear "no" is hard to give; it is difficult, even at the start of the relationship, to reject a partner directly or be rejected.

If you notice a turned-away posture, a blocking gesture of arms across the chest, or knees-drawn together, a lot of body movement, a heaviness or tiredness in the voice, lots of false starts to sentences, or hesitation and swallowed words, then you should be aware that here the message is part pull-back, part rejection. It is not a clear, definite "no."

When there is constant fidgeting and much self-touching, as if seeking comfort by rubbing the cheek or putting a hand to the mouth, it probably is not a clear "no." If the nonverbal messages contradict the spoken word (a partly genuine smile with no eye-to-eye contact), mixed signals are sent, and, of course, "no" does mean "yes."

WHEEL BALANCING AND FRONT-END ALIGNMENT

Balancing wheels and aligning the front-end of a vehicle are necessary steps to ensure that the vehicle is in safe working condition. Why such emphasis on balance? Because things simply work better when they're balanced. Imbalanced things get stuck—like when one heavy kid and one thin kid are on opposite sides of a see-saw. Non-moving objects lose their balance and fall down—like a child's spinning top. Imbalanced things are unhealthy—like a diet comprised of carbohydrates and nothing else. Most importantly, imbalanced relationships often fail. Sometimes one person is happy, while the other is miserable.

Do you remember those guys on the *Ed Sullivan Show* who balanced 300 spinning dishes on wobbly poles while riding a unicycle and juggling 15 bowling balls all at the same time? That's what relationships are like.

Relationships need balance, and the most basic concept of that balance is the yes/no judgment of settling questions and disputes. In our everyday lives many of these yes/no decisions involve balancing assertiveness and aggressiveness. The balancing of these two is a tricky concept. Assertiveness is the practice of "speaking up," enabling you to obtain what is rightfully yours without using any anger. It is a concept that deserves more respect and more practice. Because of a boy's early childhood socialization processes, it is easy for males to appear assertive. Now, though, more than ever, women are making great strides toward claiming their assertiveness without feeling guilty and without using anger.

Masculine/feminine behavior differences begin at birth and are further emphasized throughout the childhood development years. These differences are part of the cause of the assertiveness/aggressiveness imbalance between the genders. With the socialization differences for girls and boys in mind, examine the following generalizations, trends and observations. Which statements do you agree/disagree with? Discuss your views with your partner and watch the action begin.

---

xx   Women hear "love" when you say "romance."
xy   Men hear "sex" when you say "romance."

xx   Women communicate to create relationships.
xy   Men communicate to gather information.

xx   Women cooperate.
xy   Men compete.

xx   Women tend to be "right-brained"/emotional, creative thinkers.
xy   Men tend to be "left-brained"/logical, compartmentalized thinkers.

xx   Women are aroused by sensation—and slowly.
xy   Men are aroused visually—and quickly.

xx   Women have been taught to hide their angry feelings.
xy   Men have been taught to hide their tender feelings.

xx   Women have been taught to suppress their aggressive side.
xy   Men have been taught to suppress their gentle side.

Prince Charming lives! Cinderella does, too! They live on in our imaginations and in our fairy tales. We can't seem to get rid of them, so why don't we try to learn what they both have to teach us about the existence of the ideal partner and the ideal relationship. Balancing is possible, despite gender differences, and there is a possibility of *living happily ever after!*

HOW TO GET IT TOGETHER FOR A DATE

Verbal communication has to start somewhere, and by far, the most successful entrance line is a question. No one can refuse to answer a question. When asking your question, make certain it is an open-ended question. Ask a question that cannot be answered with only a yes or no response. Open-ended questions allow people to answer on their own terms. They are usually questions that begin with: who, what, where, when, why or how. Open-ended questions create communication.

Remember, your goals in asking questions is to find out as much as possible about the other person early on to determine if there is a chance for a relationship between the two of you. People like people who are interested in them, therefore, asking a question as an entrance to a relationship is to your advantage.

Any question can be used, even the traditional ones such as, "Don't I know you from somewhere?" Listed below are just of few of many:

1. What time do you have?

2. Do you come here often?

3. Who are you rooting for?

4. I'm lost. Do you know where _____ is?

5. Weren't you at _____'s party a couple of weeks ago?

6. Which type of pizza do you think is best here?

7. Do you have change for a dollar?

8. Offer something: "Would you like to read this newspaper?"

People love flattery and compliments, so don't hesitate to walk directly to someone and comment on what you find attractive. The key to success is delivering a genuine and wholesome compliment, such as, "You have the most beautiful eyes. I couldn't help noticing you." "You sound so intelligent. I just had to say hi." "Your energy and smile light up this whole room." The typical response to entrance lines like these will be a big smile and a little embarrassed blushing.

For an entrance line to be successful, though, it is better to comment on the surroundings or an object in view. It puts the other person at ease and takes some pressure off them at an early stage in relationship building.

IS HE EVER GOING TO CALL?

One of the most stressful parts about meeting someone new is waiting to see whether he is actually going to follow through with his statement, "I'll call you," with a call. For some reason, there seems to be unwritten guidelines that men feel they should follow about returning calls.

When a man meets a woman he likes, the first thing he wants to do is call her, but he stops himself. He knows that if he calls too soon or too often, he will appear overly anxious. If he waits too long then the woman might be upset and won't be anxious to go out with him. By far the most accurate rule men follow is the "two-day" rule. When a man wants to make the best impression on a woman, he will wait 48 hours before he calls her. It doesn't matter how well they got along when they met. Men know that if they call too soon, the woman might not be as anxious to talk with them, so they grit their teeth and wait the 48 hours.

Charted below are general guidelines about when he's likely to call. Does it make any sense to you?

WHEN HE'S LIKELY TO CALL _____

Day you met	Day he will call	Day he will ask you out for
Monday	Wednesday	Upcoming weekend
Tuesday	Thursday	If he detects that you already have plans, he will say he's busy that weekend too, but would like to get together the next weekend.

Wednesday	Friday afternoon	He'll leave a message saying he'll call you early next week about getting together.
Thursday	Sunday afternoon	Upcoming weekend
Friday	Sunday afternoon	Upcoming weekend
Saturday	Monday evening	Upcoming weekend or lunch during the week
Sunday	Tuesday	Upcoming weekend or lunch during the week

Most men often call on Sunday afternoon or evening because it is the least threatening night to call. Some men don't follow any rules at all, thank goodness. Those are usually the ones who have the confidence to know it's all right to chase you.

Some will never call though. When someone we've truly wanted to call us, doesn't call, the hurt we've all felt can best be expressed in these personal, private words:

It will be two weeks tomorrow,
I made it through two Saturday nights,
so far . . . almost

It hurts like hell,
But I'm going to beat it this time.

I go out every night now
I have to, for a while,
I can still smell him on the pillowcase
and even now, heat rises from his side of the covers.

I'll make it this time.
I've been careful to stay away from the radio,
one song can ambush me with a memory.

In the morning, it'll be two weeks since he said,
"I'll call soon." But, you know what,
soon's all gone now! Damn!

4 I Want a Man With a Slow Hand

TOUCH. Even the word alone sounds sexy. It can be done slowly, deliberately, gently, sensitively, seductively or flirtatiously—and is probably the first of our senses to develop. When we touch and are touched, we give a message far more immediate than any words or looks could express.

Every square inch of your body is sensitive to touch. Some parts of ourselves we touch in public, at random and with permission: our hair, hands, forearms, necks, and faces. Other skin surfaces we stroke or rub when in a particular mood: our foreheads when we are thinking; the lower back when we are stressed; the stomach when we are anxious. But sexual self-touch also takes place in public, and is an integral part of courtship behavior.

Preening is a way of flattering ourselves and flirting with others simultaneously. Both men and women preen themselves alone, often as part of the dressing to go out ritual. Once in the presence of the opposite sex, they begin to preen again. The most common preening gestures include: touching the hair with hands, comb or brush; touching the face (normally with fingertips) in brief stroking gestures, including wiping the eyebrows; touching the lips, stroking the cheeks, and smoothing the beard or mustache.

Out on the town, true preeners glance at their reflections whenever they get the chance. Women frequently check their make-up and some men glance backwards as they pass full-length mirrors to examine their appearance for flaws.

When we are attracted to someone we unconsciously fuss over our appearance. We send nonverbal sexual signals to another person by preening in their direction, usually by flicking our hair back from our face and running a hand through it while simultaneously casting a glance towards our target. We brush imaginary fluff from our shoulders, pick at invisible specks of dust on our clothes and endlessly rearrange our whole attire. During this rearranging, we rub our hands over the surface of the material of our clothing, smooth out our skirts, pull at our cuffs, readjust our ties, and so on.

If the clothes we are wearing are made from fine, sensuous material, especially silk, satin or velvet, we may arouse ourselves with their touch against our skin. By rubbing our hands up and down our clothes or our skin, we sometimes mimick what we hope we will be able to do to another person, or we delicately deliver to them a message showing where we would like to be touched.

We stroke our wrists and hands against our forearms, particularly if bare-skinned. We sometimes rub the outside of our upper thighs and then may even stroke them on the inside. Women put their hands into the back pockets of their pants and between their legs more often than men do. Women can even squeeze a hand comfortingly between folded legs and, if wearing trousers, may sit with their legs open, with a hand dropped between their legs acting as a modest fig leaf.

Women unconsciously stroke the upper part of their breasts, as if to pat off lint. This auto-erotic signaling, as the self-touch display and preening behavior is sometimes called, is a forerunner to the touching of another person. These pre-touch stages are the "readiness" part of pre-sexual interaction. We are preparing ourselves mentally and physically for a possible sexual encounter.

Once we are ready, we demonstrate our readiness for others to see. This explains the often unnecessary self-preening we do in public. This knowledge may be used to recognize potential partners and can broadcast the nonverbal message, "I'm doing this for me and maybe for you too . . ."

REACH OUT AND TOUCH

Delicately touching, smoothly caressing, or sensitively massaging someone, makes for a dramatic escalation of emotional intimacy in any relationship. To touch someone is to move physically beyond their intimate space zone barrier, and to invite touch is to make yourself accessible and vulnerable. This takes trust and courage and suggests that attraction is growing between the two of you.

A couple, on their first date, is aware and nervous of the first obvious touch. Getting the timing right can be quite difficult. As a result, they may begin by brushing against each other, accidentally on purpose, which makes the step to deliberate touching that much easier. Sometimes while walking next to each other, the backs of their hands will touch for a moment. What happens next is crucial. If either person wishes, they can withdraw their hand to another position ensuring no further touching, or they can ensure that the touch is repeated so as to lead to holding hands.

The first intimate touch is usually hand to hand. It's not the formal handshake, but often a brief, apparently accidental touch. Women, as well as men, are just as capable of initiating touch. We should all be aware, though, that to initiate a touch is the first physical signal of "I'm attracted to you."

How and when you first touch obviously depends on your situation. If you are going to rush across a busy road together, you may instinctively join hands as you step into the street. You may suddenly want to point out something in a shop window and grab your companion enthusiastically. As intimacy increases and attraction levels rise, courting couples touch each other with increasing frequency. These touches can be momentary, as with joking little slaps or pushes used during an animated story, or more sensuous strokes of the arms, face or hair. A hand placed on the back of the other person can be used to guide them or draw them closer.

Parties are ideal places for the first physical contact, allowing people to touch by dancing together, fast or slowly. Dancing accelerates the normal progressive stages of acceptable touch. Other than at a party or on a dance floor, deviation from the normal sequence of advances can cause annoyance and anxiety.

The simple act of passing any object to a person presents you with the chance to touch or to be touched. Whether you are handing over a pen, offering someone a light for a cigarette, or helping a woman as she puts on her coat, a connection is made.

Even one brief touch has a profound effect on the way we feel towards someone. We can all think back to that first brief touch we received from someone we admired, and it still renews fleeting memories of passion, desire and positive feelings within us. Research reports that waiters and waitresses who touch their customers gently, are likely to be given larger gratuities.

This "anchoring" should create a positive feeling in other people, connecting them to you physically and you to them. It gives you added status; you hold the authority and self-confidence to "reach out and touch," and it implies that you trust this person enough to risk touching. The really important point is that by moving into another person's intimate personal space, you are bringing him or her into yours too.

The sincerest sign of attraction is to preen or groom someone else or have them groom you. To pick a piece of lint from another person's jacket or shirt is completely harmless, yet provides great potential for intimacy and is a sure way to reveal to others that you have, "staked your claim."

When you're involved in a nonverbal exchange with someone, keep reading their signs to check for invitations or acceptance of touch. If you do touch, check their responses. If you both feel comfortable and right, then continue. But, if the other person withdraws or tenses up, or if the nonverbal signals change abruptly, release your hold on them and give them more space. Keep your body language warm and positive, but be aware of how much personal space the other person needs to feel safe. What you want to avoid is a negative cascade of awkward feelings and misunderstandings.

Placing an arm around someone's waist is a very intimate act. If you time it right, it will be accepted and enjoyed. If you time it wrong, you may create tension or even provoke rejection. When someone is ready for you to put your arm around his or her waist or shoulder, he or she will stand so close to you that your hips will brush together. Your arms will no longer have room to swing, and instead will hang awkwardly, knocking against each other. This is the moment to make your move, especially if the other person has turned his or her torso slightly towards you.

RESERVED PARKING: TOUCHING EACH OTHER

Following is a list of the usual sequence of touching escalation:

1. Hand to hand

2. Hand to forearm

3. Linked arms

4. Hand to shoulder

5. Arm around waist

6. Hand to hair/head

7. Hand to back, neck

8. Hands around each other's waists

9. Hands rubbing up and down each other's backs

10. Hands holding face and kissing begins

S ENSITIVE, SEDUCTIVE, SOOTHING HANDS

Hands signal intimate feelings and perform three main roles in sexual nonverbal communication: they touch, point, and signal. We can draw in the air with them, indicate when we wish to speak with them, and we can even call a crowd to silence just by touching a finger to our lips. Such is the power that lies in our fingertips.

TOUCH

Each aspect of touch—pressure, speed and rhythm—can be seen to carry a subtly different message. A light, soft touch with little pressure may signal erotic teasing. Touch, though, usually becomes firmer and heavier as passion increases. Slow speed and regular rhythm signal relaxation or reassurance. With desire, speed increases, and the rhythm becomes irregular to create amorous interest.

The key to seductive, soothing hand talk is matching movement to need. If you know that your partner's need is for comfort and security, a firm, steady touch is best. Light, soft, slow touches, moving gradually into stronger, more rhythmical touches are appealing when desire begins to rise.

POINT

"Don't point, it's rude!" How many times were you told this as a child? Frequently, probably, but it is a highly contradictory command. As children we learn that it is impolite to point at people; as adults we realize that we do like pointing at things we want. We point at the most scrumptious-looking chocolate desserts and say, "I'll have some of that, please!" Well, the same is true when it comes to sexual desire. We love to point at our prospective love and at our own best assets as part of our courtship ritual. Sometimes we point with our finger in the gun position, to indicate to another that we have chosen them. It is as powerful as actually throwing a line to them. We can use a pointing signal over a long distance, especially in conjunction with a smile or an eyebrow flash, to let someone know that we are interested.

We can also point more inconspicuously, when we vaguely motion in someone's direction, using a glass, sunglasses or even an umbrella. By simply using our hands and arms, we can point to someone in such a way as to invite them to join us or to indicate that we are having a conversation about them.

Often, without realizing it, we will point to our genitals. It is a very charged, nonverbal signal and is more often performed by men. Crotch-pointing can be implied when men use the "cowpoke" stance. Even pushing a hand into a pocket is suggestive because the viewer's eye is automatically drawn down the arm in search of the hand.

The "cowpoke" stance can take various forms. A man's thumbs can be hooked into the tops of his trousers, his belt, his belt loop or his pockets and anywhere from one finger to four may do the actual pointing. One or both hands placed on your hips can also point towards your genitals. The angle of the arms, in this type of stance, makes a big difference between masculine and feminine gesture signals.

The classic stance of the gunslinger about to draw his pistol is still used in advertising posters to sell macho products and also by male and female stars for a special effect. During performances, Madonna and Prince both point to their sexual assets. Some women will hunch their shoulders forward so as to increase the apparent fullness of their breasts and the depth of their cleavage.

We also use our hands and fingers to point to our eyes and mouths, both of which are highly sexually communicative features of our faces.

SIGNALS

We signal our attraction with our hands in several ways. When we greet someone there is often a handshake. A firm handshake (where web touches web) is most desirable for both men and women, but a handshake any longer than five seconds will imply a desire for greater intimacy.

A gentle tug can signal attraction, and even the slightest squeeze on the fleshy part of the palm can make a person of either sex squirm, or want to have you hold his or her hand for a longer period of time. Leaning gently forward while shaking hands increases arousal and makes intimacy intentions more clear.

A very fleshy Mount of Venus, the part of the palm at the base of the thumb, is claimed by some to indicate high sensuality, and the supporters of palmistry will agree that the lines on our hands reveal information about our character, personality, careers, destiny, luck and relationships. Whether you are a believer or not, asking to read someone else's palm is one of the most common and transparent excuses many newly courting couples use in trying to touch each other's hands for the first time. (See section in this chapter on "How Many Marriages? How Many Children?")

We use our hands to signal interest in someone by moving them into another person's space. We edge our hands forward across the surface of a table or bar. We reveal open palms, which are friendly and inviting, towards the person we desire as a peaceful gesture of goodwill or as a signal aimed at further suggestive touching.

Wrists have always been considered highly erotic, especially on women, and to this day, the display of the wrist is highly sensual and arousing. Women sprinkle their wrists with perfume and gently throw their hands back and palms upward when asking for help to get a cigarette lit.

Maybe this is the reason why wristwatches play such a role in flirting manners and successful opening lines begin with, "Do you know what time it is?" Another use of the inner wrist is in the yawning stretch— lift your arms up, out and in front of you, making certain that both your wrists are facing towards the other person. And, why is it that women look so dreamy and sexy, when they tilt their heads to one side and rest their chin in a cupped hand? Is the wrist not exposed then, too? Exaggerated wrist displays and limp-wrist gestures are supreme examples of femininity.

Often, very suggestively, hands are used to caress inanimate objects. The objects, usually phallic in shape, may hint at a secret romantic act we may be daydreaming about, as we talk with someone we find sexually interesting. The rhythm with which someone rubs on their keys or covers and uncovers their eyes with a pair of sunglasses, provides onlookers with a sort of implied striptease.

A dinner table provides plenty opportunities for selecting phallic objects, ranging from the ever present candle to the pieces of delicate silverware, the wine bottle, the stem of a wine glass, the pepper grinder and many others. We often use our hands to play with these objects at the dinner table, sometimes in motions similar to sensual movements. We even use our hands, and especially our fingers, to mimic erotic movements as we lick or suck food from them.

HANDLING FLIRTATIOUS DRINKS

There is no better accessory at a party than a glass in your hand. It gives your hands something to do, which tends to calm you down, and the activities surrounding drinking (nonalcoholic or alcoholic) are a flirting ritual in themselves.

Here are some guidelines for making the most of your opportunities to flirt while enjoying liquid refreshment.

1. *Long, cool drinks are flirtatious.* So is anything that can be stirred or mixed or shaken. This implies that you are going to be there for a while, which helps take the pressure off the situation. Giving a hurried appearance is never a good idea.

2. *For women flirts, a straw is one of the best accessories imaginable.* You can twirl it or dip it, but for goodness sake, don't take it out and begin to chew on it. Chewing on a straw is a sign that you need nourishment, not in the way of food, but in the way of words or love. (It can either mean that you have nothing to say, or that you are starved for love!)

3. *For men flirts, it is best not to gulp a drink or down it too quickly. And never order anything with an umbrella in it.* If by mistake you do get the umbrella, put it and the fruit aside immediately. But, all is not lost. You might offer them to your female flirting partner—this is considered by women to be a nice, friendly gesture. Serious male flirts should stay away from those ultra-feminine, overly gimmicky drinks.

4. *If you are ever in a place that serves free champagne, order a regular drink from the menu.* This sets you apart. It proves that you're not one of the people who are eating a tasteless brunch just so you can sip all that free, cheap champagne.

5. *Drinking beer out of a gigantic mug is out.* This is definitely not flirtatious for women for two reasons: Women look like weight lifters when they lift the mug, and a gigantic mug doesn't give a man an opening to offer a drink. (Why should he? You have enough beer for the whole evening.) Successful women flirts never order pitchers or regular bottles of wine for that reason.

6. *Male flirts who drink beer should never put a two-quart pitcher on the table.* It acts as a psychological barrier when women approach. And, men who drink beer are sexier and more appealing drinking it out of a glass. If glasses are not available, cans are certainly more flirtatious than bottles. They tend to squeeze their beer cans to indicate when they'd like to squeeze you.

7. *Flirts of both sexes should stay away from short drinks.* And, particularly stay away from having a shot of anything. (What's your hurry?) Wine is always good. It implies a bit of culture— a plus in every way! It depicts you as a special person, and since it goes so fast, it's easy to finesse a refill. Getting a refill either from the host, bartender, or your drinking partner can be an occasion to talk, touch, and share something.

8. *Should a man offer to buy a woman a drink?* Yes. Though a man may profess to love it when a woman offers him a drink, this flirtatious gesture usually dampens a woman's chances for a relationship. It doesn't crush her chances, it only diminishes her edge on the relationship. A woman who brings wine or an after-dinner liqueur over to a man's home as a present, however, is considered not only flirtatious, but warm, caring, and definitely indicative of possible spousal material.

9. *Teetotalers can be just as flirtatious as anyone by drinking soda.* Do keep drinking along with the others. Every group needs someone designated to drive the others home.

HOW MANY MARRIAGES? HOW MANY CHILDREN?

There's a gypsy I know who will read your palm and answer any two questions for ten dollars. If there's anything amiss in your life, a wish that's hard to make true, she always asks for an extra ten dollars so she can burn ten candles for ten days and light your wish into reality.

I've always wondered whether she really burns the candles or if it's just a hype for more money. But either way, she has a point: wishes don't come true by wishing them once. They become completed through effort and attention and just as the gypsy lights the candles to insure results, it's holding the flame of desire in our hearts and minds, in our emotions and actions, that will bring our most heartfelt wishes into being.

While we cannot read minds, some of us can read hands and palms. To further develop my study of reading people, I've practiced the art of palm reading for the past five years, and know that the lines on your palms represent a map of your past, present and future events, and have an influence throughout your life.

Those lines are with you from birth and will deepen when events are due to arise. This gives the untrained eye the impression that a new line is developing, when, in actuality, palmists know that the line was always there, it was just very light. Taking prints of your palms, from time to time, using a photocopier, will prove this to you, as the prints will show lines you did not realize were there.

Both hands are important to a palmist, as the difference between them is important. Your left hand shows your inherited tendencies, while your right hand will show your cultivated or developed traits. I have always chosen to read the right palm of a person, because it shows exactly who they are, where they are, and the direction in which they are headed.

Compare your hand and your partner's hand to the drawing below for indications concerning your marriage line or lines (there may be more than one) and your affection line. Also, pay close attention to the cross lines which indicate the number of children you will have.

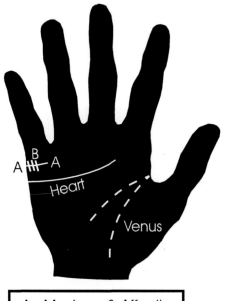

A - Marriage & Affection
B - Children

WHEN WILL A PERSON MARRY?

The marriage or affection lines appear on the palm under the little finger (they begin from the underside of the hand and go to the mid-point of the little finger). If the marriage line is down near the heart line, a person will marry early in life (or form a relationship so deep that it is like a marriage). But if it is nearer the little finger, the person will marry later in life.

HOW MANY MARRIAGES?

If there is one straight deep line, the person will marry once. The number of lines equals the number of marriages. Fine lines show affairs.

VARIATIONS OF THE AFFECTION/MARRIAGE LINES

Cuts and breaks in the marriage line show that there is a risk of jealousy breaking a marriage. A fine line running parallel to a marriage line indicates a relationship outside a marriage. If a marriage line turns down at the end and swings toward the heart line, it tells of divorce. If it curves up at the end, it indicates that the marriage will not produce children.

WILL I HAVE A GOOD LOVE LIFE?

The shape and direction of the heart line is the clue to the love life. If the heart line ends under the:

   a. pointer finger, it shows a person who will be very idealistic and ambitious in his love life; he's a conqueror, and likes to take charge of everything.

   b. between the pointer finger and the middle finger, it indicates the person has a forgiving nature and is sometimes too gullible; this type tends to fall in love casually and easily.

   c. middle finger, it indicates that more than love will be needed to keep the marriage going. This type needs a mate with many like interests and is usually seeking a very intelligent partner.

   d. ring finger, the person will be more of a mental companion, rather than a spouse. This type is usually very judgmental, very analytical, and looks for perfection in others.

   e. little finger, it is a sign of selfishness and emotional detachment. This type is satisfied staying single, and a hard catch to land.

HOW TO TELL HOW SENSUAL A PERSON WILL BE?

The section below the thumb, which is the Mount of Venus and named after the goddess of love, indicates the sensual nature of a person. The more well developed, fleshier and firmer the mount, the more romantic and sensual the person will be. If the mount is quite flat, the relationship may be short on passion and, therefore, require a lot of encouragement. Several vertical lines on the Mount of Venus indicates a huge need for affection.

HOW MANY CHILDREN?

The number of children a person will have is marked by the fine lines that start at the base of the little finger and run down through the marriage line or lines. Each line is a potential child. Deep lines will be boys and fine lines will be girls. A line that starts as one and becomes two, is a sign of twins. If the lines are at the beginning (towards the underneath of the palm) of the marriage line, the children will be born in the first few years of marriage. If they are further along the line (moving towards the middle of the little finger), children will not arrive until later on.

Go ahead, try your luck at palm reading. It's a great way to create a bond between you and someone else. Touching implies a connection between two people and social psychologists believe that touching does lead to liking.

MAKING THE MOVES

In the process of getting together, every move we make counts. We try to develop empathy, create rapport and ultimately advance to synergy. It is a sobering thought that everything we do at this early stage makes the difference between success and failure. It is an even more sobering thought that everything our potential partner does also makes or breaks the situation. Together we win or lose.

He laughs, and she relaxes; she relaxes, so he feel more confident; he feels more confident, so she begins to confide; she confides, and he holds her hand to comfort her. They move forward in tandem. Yet every few minutes something could go wrong. With every small interaction, there could be a potential hazard. His initial laugh could, completely unintentionally, sound like mockery; she might tense as a result; sensing her tension, he may withdraw, and soon she will decide that she has to go home early.

We normally manage to prevent such disasters. If we can sense them before they happen, we can move quickly to correct the damage as each one occurs. For example, if she does feel threatened when he laughs, and he notices, he will rush to reassure her, openly or without words. This time the situation is saved, and they can move forward again.

EMPATHY

Empathy is the term often used to describe the ability to be able to view a situation or problem from someone else's point of view. Successful empathy, similar to the kind necessary in counseling, depends on exceptionally sensitive responses to the body language of others. This heightened awareness of another person's movements can provide increased success in potential seductive encounters.

People astute in the nonverbal communication of romance can take the lead in timing and synchronization and produce desired results from those who interest them. Since their intended role is to draw others out, to reinforce and reassure, they know that a liberal use of positive head tilts and direct eye contact will help to encourage conversation and interest.

RAPPORT

If successful communication is to take place between you and someone else, rapport must be established. For this to happen, you need clear channels of communication, some degree of trust in, and acceptance of, the other person and a smooth pattern of interaction.

There are several things you can do to create rapport. You can use a warm, friendly manner, together with lots of genuine smiles and eye contact. Treating the other person as an equal is the most powerful tool for successful rapport. Finding a common interest or experience, giving another your full attention, or making it clear that there is plenty of time for the encounter, also help to establish rapport.

When everything is working in your favor, postures will be forward, bodily contact will often be appropriate and movements begin to be imitated.

SYNERGY 2 + 2 = 5

Synergy is the phenomenon which sometimes occurs, whereby the outcome of a situation is greater than the sum of the parts. It is sometimes described by the formula $2 + 2 = 5$. Examples of synergy might include the performance of a play that is not just good, but gets several curtain calls from an elated audience; the football team which does not merely win its matches, but seems as if it cannot lose; or the party at which every part is better than best.

Nonverbally, synergy is promoted by sensitive timing and synchronization. When things are going so well and with such a rhythm that an occasion acquires a dimension of magic and a sense of being special, you've created synergy. When an artist gives such a perfectly timed and paced performance that it is absolutely flawless, that too is synergy.

Synergy begins on a personal level by cautious and intentional eye contact, head movement, gestures, postures and nonverbal aspects of speech. Incidents need to work together exceptionally well for synergy to be produced. When it happens, it adds an extra quality well worth striving for.

USE CAUTION: SOUL MAN ON BOARD

Falling in love is often associated with synergy and the mysterious feeling of being on the same wavelength, a wordless understanding between virtual strangers. But this shared wavelength is really not so mysterious—it is simply a sensory connection between two people who relate to the world in the same way. That connection can happen spontaneously—or you can create it.

Grammar school teachers have known for years that children learn by seeing, hearing and touching. Since three of our human senses are sight, sound and touch, knowing your mate's dominant sense will reveal the basis of his personality and his inner "love language." Understood and used properly, this information can be the key to his heart.

In order to fully understand your mate, try walking a mile in your sweetheart's shoes. Walking a mile in your sweetheart's shoes means being able to see around the corner of your own assumptions and discover how he actually experiences the world. Determine if your mate is a "seeing," "hearing," or "feeling" type by listening with an open ear and a non-judgmental heart to the unspoken. This insight will allow you to speak and act in certain ways that will rivet his attention, and make him feel as if you are his soul mate. Even the most elusive lover can be put under your spell with this information.

If you have trouble identifying your partner's type, if his boots are too big or her glass slipper only has room for your big toe, here's an exercise for both of you to try:

LOVE LANGUAGE SELF-TEST _____

1. Given $1,000 to spend on one of the following, which would your choose?

   a. A new mattress

   b. A new stereo

   c. A new television

      Her _____   Him _____

2. Which would you rather do?

   a. Stay home and eat a home-cooked meal

   b. Go out to a concert

   c. Go to a movie

      Her _____   Him _____

3. Given a choice of activities at a resort, which would you choose?

   a. Going to a lecture

   b. Exploring hiking trails

   c. Relaxing and doing nothing

      Her _____   Him _____

4. Which of these rooms would you most enjoy?

   a. One with a terrific view

   b. One with an ocean breeze

   c. One in a quiet corner

      Her _____   Him _____

5. To which event would you rather go?

   a. A wedding

   b. An art exhibit

   c. A cocktail party

      Her _____   Him _____

6. Which are you considered?

   a. Athletic

   b. Intellectual

   c. Humanitarian

   Her _____   Him _____

7. How do you most often keep in touch?

   a. By talking on the phone

   b. By writing letters

   c. By having lunch

   Her _____   Him _____

8. How do you prefer to spend quality time with your mate?

   a. Talking

   b. Touching

   c. Watching

   Her _____   Him _____

9. If you lost your keys, what would you do?

   a. Look for them

   b. Shake your pocketbook or pockets to hear them jingle

   c. Feel around for them

   Her _____   Him _____

10. If you were going to be stranded on a desert island, what would you most want to take along?

    a. Some good books

    b. A portable radio

    c. Your sleeping bag

    Her _____   Him _____

11. Which type of dresser are you?

    a. Immaculate

    b. Casual

    c. Laid back

    Her _____   Him _____

12. Which of these would you rather be?

    a. In the know

    b. Very chic

    c. Comfortable

    Her _____   Him _____

13. If you have unlimited money, what would you do?

    a. Buy a great house and stay there

    b. Travel and see the world

    c. Join the social scene

    Her _____   Him _____

14. If you could, which would you rather be?

    a. A great doctor

    b. A great musician

    c. A great artist

    Her _____   Him _____

15. Which do you think is sexier?

    a. Soft lighting

    b. Perfume

    c. Specific music

    Her _____   Him _____

ANSWERS:

1.	a) feelings	b) auditory	c) visual
2.	a) feelings	b) auditory	c) visual
3.	a) auditory	b) visual	c) feelings
4.	a) visual	b) feelings	c) auditory
5.	a) feelings	b) visual	c) auditory
6.	a) visual	b) auditory	c) feelings

7. a) auditory	b) visual	c) feelings
8. a) auditory	b) feelings	c) visual
9. a) visual	b) auditory	c) feelings
10. a) visual	b) auditory	c) feelings
11. a) visual	b) auditory	c) feelings
12. a) auditory	b) visual	c) feelings
13. a) feelings	b) visual	c) auditory
14. a) feelings	b) auditory	c) visual
15. a) visual	b) feelings	c) auditory

Count the number of visual, auditory and feelings preferences for both you and your mate. The area that has the most answers is your primary Love Language, the next highest area is your secondary Love Language, and the third is your least active Love Language.

ROAD RULES: STOP, LOOK AND LISTEN

A man stays in love when he feels you understand him completely, and love him anyway. When a man feels that he can communicate with you like he can with no one else, you become irreplaceable to him. And, when you know the secrets that can change his moods and create intimacy, he's not just in love—he's crazy about you.

Your man's unconscious preference for one particular sense affects his personality and inner thoughts. He is more "tuned in" and receptive in this one sense; you've discovered his wavelength, in other words, his Love Language, therefore, learn it and use it to your advantage.

THE VISUAL MAN

A Visual Man relates to the world in terms of how everything looks to him. When he's remembering something from the past, he'll recall a picture. When he's imagining something in the future, he'll visualize it. He usually prefers face-to-face meetings instead of long phone calls, and he will respond better to written messages than to spoken ones. If you want to be sure he remembers something, write him a note.

He's often described as a "type A" personality who has high energy and lots of interests. He's quick moving and as long as he has something interesting to look at, he'll be happy. Your Visual Man is very organized and likes his world neat and tidy. He's always checking things to make sure they're right. When he drives a car, he looks in the rear-view mirror a lot and watches the other drivers carefully. He always likes to have lots of maps and if you are giving him directions, it's best to draw a map instead of writing them out.

He can sometimes become moody or difficult if he's overwhelmed with too much auditory stimulation, such as loud music or continual chatter. He prefers talking about how things look; talking about how he feels can make him very uncomfortable. He finds it difficult to communicate his feelings, but that doesn't mean that he's insensitive, unfeeling or unemotional.

When he's angry, he's likely to clam up and give you the silent treatment rather than rant and rave. Since it's very hard for him to express emotions, you may have to learn to express them for him, or at least help him by asking questions in his visual language.

Getting Intimate with Your Visual Man

To let a visual man know how much you love him, write him a note or buy him things that he will see. Give him pictures of the two of you looking lovingly at each other. Your Visual Man will be excited by what he sees. He loves to see you looking good. Ask him, "What color do you think *looks* best on me?" Look through a catalog together and ask him what he thinks of different outfits.

When you approach your Visual Man, always give him lots of time to look first. Don't rush up and hug him the second he walks in, give him a chance to see you. Visual men like all kinds of visual signs of affection and sensual interest. Say things like, "Your shoulders look sexy in that shirt," or "I can picture us lying in the warm sun together." He is also going to be turned on by a special look from you. If there's a specific expression you make that he can't resist, give him a picture for his desk, and one for his wallet; give him lots of visual signs of your love. He usually likes to make love with the lights on and kisses with his eyes open; he wants to stop and look before he does anything. Wearing something sexy is a definite *do*.

THE AUDITORY MAN

The Auditory Man is more in tune with the inner logic of words than with feelings. He is articulate, expresses himself well, likes long conversations and enjoys debating almost any issue. His feelings are triggered by what he hears and he remembers what he hears better than others do. The Auditory Man tends to be laid back and relates better to music than to pictures.

His favorite activities are reading, doing projects, listening to music and talking. He doesn't have to run around to see what's happening, and would rather hear about an incident than have to see it for himself. He's very cerebral and sometimes has conversations with himself, in his own head. There are two types of Auditory Men. One is always playing the stereo (never adjust the radio in his car or home; he has it just like he likes it), talking, or filling the silences in one way or another. The other kind of auditory person seems, at times, to hate any sounds at all (often when he's working or trying to concentrate). He feels that any sound is an interruption of the conversation he's already having with himself.

When shopping for anything, he'd rather make lots of phone calls instead of driving around to find the best deal. If you want him to remember something, just tell him. He likes to explain everything in detail. Even when it comes to his feelings, he tends to be more analytical than sympathetic. Rather than express a feeling, he'll start analyzing the situation and try to come up with several possible solutions to the problem he's faced with.

He's not very particular about how things look. He'll wear the clothes you pick out for him and let you choose the decor at home. The best way to let an Auditory Man know you love him is to tell him as often as possible. He needs to hear you say it over and over again. If you don't have pet names for him, think of some. If you don't have special little things you say to him, make some up.

Getting Intimate with Your Auditory Man

Your auditory lover is more concerned with how things sound than with how they look. That means if he's coming over, set up a stack of CDs and turn the music on before you worry about cleaning up your place. Actually, he's pretty easy to keep happy; you just have to say the right words and make the right noises. Say things like, "The sound of your voice turns me on," or "It's great how our bodies seem in tune for each other." Try talking dirty to him and he'll be eating out of the palm of your hand. He wants to know you love him, and he wants to know it in a way he can hear. Let him know what you like and tell him how sexy he is. The more you talk to him, the more excited he'll get.

THE FEELINGS MAN

The Feelings Man is sensitive and wears his heart on his sleeve. He will be the first to get hurt in a relationship. He will wait for his heart to tell him it's love, and you can't rush him. For him to be in love, the relationship has to feel right, but not only in his heart, all over his body. The Feelings Man responds to the loving touch and greets people with hearty handshakes. He enjoys food and drink and loves physical pleasures such as kisses and hugs.

The Feelings Man is the easiest of men to communicate with. He is a man who cries easily, is emotional and sometimes is easily upset. Fortunately, he's quick to make up after he cools off. When he's happy, he wants to share it with everyone around him. His smile seems to light up the room and nobody can resist him. His feelings show all the time; he looks at you and love shows in his eyes; he talks to you and you hear love in his voice.

Physical comfort is important to the Feelings Man. He likes everything he touches to feel good, so he'll love you in soft velvets, cashmeres and smooth silks. He tends to be very athletic and likes to jog or work out. This usually leaves him with a good excuse to ask for a sensual back rub. He is more spontaneous than the Visual or Auditory Man and likes to do things on the spur of the moment.

The Feelings Man craves close physical proximity to his mate and craves love and affection. He's sensitive to the way you touch him, or don't touch him, and to how you do or don't respond to his touch.

Getting Intimate with Your Feelings Man

Hugs, kisses and tender touches will make him respond with plenty of love. Don't be shy. Throw your arms around him, rub up against him. Say things like, "I love the way your body feels," or "I want you to hold me tightly." The Feelings Man is also certain to be intense about his senses of taste and smell. Find out his favorite perfume, then bathe yourself with it. Feed him grapes with your fingers. Massage him all over with baby oil and he'll purr like a kitten. Experiment. He'll love whatever you do, as long as it feels good.

IT TAKES TWO TO TANGO

It does take two to tango. Women have a Love Language of their own, and also need to know whether they are primarily a Seeing, Hearing, or Feeling person. Chances are it's not the same as your mate's. It doesn't have to be for the two of you to have a harmonious relationship, but it is very important that you learn what your Love Language is. When you do, you will have a whole new understanding of how and why you and he react differently, love differently and experience things differently. Knowing and accepting your mate's Love Language and your own, allows for a perfect tango between two people in love.

MOVING IN THE FAST LANE: SO YOU WANT TO BE A STAR

"All it takes is a good wake-up call in L.A. to change your life," states a 22-year-old New York University budding actor. That's the kind of relentless optimism which billows through the famous film-making city daily. From an actor's perspective though, careers in acting just seem to keep getting shorter. The circle of stardom—fame, overexposure and backlash—is spinning faster than ever. It's always, "Do I look right?" And, if you do; you're hot and you own the town.

Stars possess charisma. That's what makes them stars and makes them stand out in the crowd. It's difficult to define, but it seems to be a quality that some people have which draws others' eyes to them. Charisma causes actors to be raised on to a pedestal in the popular mind. Successful stars learn just how to incorporate empathy, rapport and synergy into their characters. The perfect union of these key ingredients is "charisma."

Charisma is most common in leaders, entertainers and sports personalities, but it is also present to some degree in many of the people you might meet in the course of an average day. The old man in the pub who is a "bit of a character" has charisma. So does the captain of the school football team, the lifeguard, the homecoming queen, the basketball coach, the society maven, and so on.

Our everyday experiences tell us that there are many good singers, actors, dancers, and comedians, but only a few of them become stars. Clearly, luck plays a part. But, certain body language is also crucial to star quality.

How do charismatic personalities use body language? They're dominant, rather than submissive, in their mannerisms. Stars will gaze longer and have more intense eye contact with others. For some stars, increased eye contact is the most important aspect of body language. They love to look, and especially to be looked at. They blossom in the limelight of others' attention. They feed upon it, thrive upon it and beam at their audiences.

Stars smile and grin a great deal. Their facial expressions are always fast-changing and expressive or sullen and seductive. A common head movement of stars is to toss the head backwards. It usually occurs during pauses in a song or when taking the audience's applause as if to allow everyone as clear a view as possible.

Gestures and posture are vital to the success of actors and stars. They must appear open, therefore, their hands are frequently palm up, with the arms stretching out as if to embrace the audience or to bring the spectators into the interaction. Their gestures are often self-manipulative. They're constantly stroking their hair, straightening their clothes or seductively exposing their bodies for all to see.

Stars are nearly always people you "look at but do not touch," therefore, body contact is infrequent. Their appearance is almost always highly attractive or highly unusual. Their timing, movements and synchronism are sharp and dominant because they're quite aware that there must be things about them which distinguish them from others. They must be remembered to be successful; therefore, they've acquired successful ways to empathize well with others, they've learned how to develop cohesive rapport with their admirers, and they've mastered the importance of establishing synergy with their audiences. Some of the aspects of body language which accompany star quality can be incorporated into our everyday actions to enhance our own attractiveness.

Become your own "star!" Tap into your own inner characters and have fun. Learn to be creative, playful and different. Why not let people recognize your wonderful charm and charisma? Express yourself, revel in your uniqueness, your own quirkiness, your eccentricity. Wear sneakers with a tuxedo. Wear a crown at home while doing your housework. Eccentrics have a tendency to look at the world just a little differently from everyone else.

We all have our own cast of inner characters, but most of us are out of touch with them. We're either scared of them, embarrassed by others, or we've forgotten about some of them. I've named my characters in a sort-of generic but descriptive way. There's the Free Spirit, the Intellectual, the Fool, the Princess and 5-year-old Little Jill who lives inside me. I even sometimes admit other of my inner characters, such as the Mother, the Catholic School Girl, and the Sailor. We all have both masculine and feminine sides to our psyches, and if you can tap into them when you need to, it makes you a better actor—and perhaps a healthier, more well-balanced human being.

Whether you're John Wayne, Blondie, or the Wicked Witch of the West, this lighthearted approach to your inner souls can cast some serious light on your personality. This intimate search can also be helpful in understanding your partner. Try this:

1. Be wacky. List your own cast of inner characters. Go for it.

2. Read your list to your lover and ask him/her to add any character that you'd rather forget, or that you're just blind to.

3. Which characters does your partner love? Hate? Tolerate? Fear?

Your life is either a celebration or a chore. The choice is yours to be unique, express yourself, and love yourself. Live out all of your characters while you have the opportunity. Bring them home and have fun with them. Waltz into the kitchen door wearing your crown and proudly announce, "Honey, I'm back. I could have gone somewhere else, but I'm here!" Or, purring slowly, quote Hungarian beauty Zsa Zsa Gabor when she said, "Dahling, can't you tell I'm a great housekeeper? After every divorce, I keep the house."

S EXUAL HEALING

Sex alone will not sustain a relationship, intimacy will. Intimacy fuels, enhances and drives a successful relationship. Intimacy, made up of emotional closeness, physical closeness and spiritual closeness, is the bond that ensures a relationship will just keep getting better and better.

Each partner brings energy and synergy, both positive and negative to a relationship, to keep it going. The more positive and honest the vibes are, the more healthy the relationship will be. The energy we bring comes from caring, trust, support and communication. These constitute the ingredients for true intimacy and sexual healing.

Being honest, supportive and fair enables people to be close emotionally. People who feel loved and worthy of being loved enjoy greater peace of mind, have a higher level of self-esteem, and possess a more effective immune system, than those who feel unworthy and unlovable. Being and staying in love is healthy. "Kissing doesn't last, cooking does." "Living happily ever after" does have its benefits; it has been reported that couples involved in a healthy relationship live longer than people who are not involved in a healthy relationship or live alone.

Are you sending healthy sexual vibes? Grab your mate and find out. Guess what? You may be exuding spectacular waves of sensual energy without even knowing it! (Maybe that's why your partner is always so excited to see you.) To discover how high-voltage you and your mate actually are, take the following his-and-hers, true/false quiz and find out!

FOR HER

1. I own fewer than five nighties.   T   F

2. Although I could open my own candle boutique, I can never resist buying just one more.   T   F

3. I believe using the right mood music can intensify a romantic experience.   T   F

4. I'll usually touch acquaintances in a friendly manner sometime during our conversation.   T   F

5. I feel naked when I'm not wearing any perfume.   T   F

6. I've cultivated a low, dreamy voice so I can leave a personal greeting on my answering machine.   T   F

7. Sometimes I pout like a child to get my own way.   T   F

8. I have no inhibitions about walking around in public with wet hair.   T   F

9. I work out religiously to keep my body fit and tight.   T   F

10. I'll spend the last of my paycheck to get my nails done.   T   F

11. When it's just my lover and me within ear shot, I'll whisper sexy words to him.   T   F

FOR HIM

1. I own at least one set of black silk sheets.   T   F

2. Two of my favorite colors are fire red and midnight blue.   T   F

3. Like James Bond, I'll order a martini over a beer.   T   F

4. I've asked my partner to wear short skirts and plunging necklines to please me.   T   F

5. I've already fed my lady with my fingers while in a public restaurant.   T   F

6. I work out regularly with weights to maintain my physique.   T   F

7. So long as the weather holds up, I enjoy walking around bare to the waist in my home and in my yard.   T   F

8. I've been very vocal about my ideal vacation: a room with a view of the ocean that offers 24-hour room service.   T   F

9. My dream car has a big gear shifter, is wildly expensive and has a removable top.   T   F

10. I enjoy thumbing through a *Victoria's Secret* catalog.   T   F

11. I've prepared at least one candlelight dinner for my mate.   T   F

SCORING: HOW MUCH SEXUAL ENERGY ARE YOU GIVING?

Give yourselves each one point for every statement you answered as true.

9–11 High Voltage Wire:

You're a person who would rather party and play than settle down to serious business. You're on a sexual high and you're the reason. Try channeling some of those incredible energy waves toward making both you and your partner happy and you'll both feel fulfilled.

5–8 Electric Shock Mate:

You're a person who is sexual by nature, and you send out just the right amount of sexual vibes. Be careful though that others don't interpret your innocent flirting moves of light-hearted conversation into a more serious light.

0–4 Short Wave Partner:

You're sending out sexual vibes that fall short of their target. Perhaps afraid to be seen as the pursuer, you dress conservatively, engage in conversations that are anything but steamy, and may even think of yourself as less than desirable. This need not be; increase your voltage, learn to say, "I'm ready to play!" Your vibes will be spectacular.

D. H. Lawrence, in his poem *Women In Love*, said it best:

> *"She traced with her hands the line of his loins and thighs,*
> *at the back, and a living fire ran through her, from him, darkly.*
>
> *It was a dark flood of electric passion she released from him,*
> *drew into herself. She had established a rich new circuit,*
> *a new current of passional electric energy,*
> *between the two of them.*
>
> *'My love,' she cried, lifting her face to him, her eyes,*
> *her mouth open in transport.*
>
> *'My love,' he answered, bending and kissing her,*
> *always kissing her."*

Just Want Your Extra Time, and Your Kiss

 ISS AND TELL

IF you could kiss—but only kiss—one person you know anytime, anywhere you wanted, who would it be?

IF you had to select the sexiest word in the English language, what would you say it is?

IF you could give someone a hickey in any shape and size, who would receive it?

IF you were to talk about the greatest lips you have ever kissed, how would you describe them?

IF you had to guess the person you work with who is likely to wear sexy underwear, who would it be?

IF you could have one part of your body glow in the dark, what part would it be?

IF you were to continue the quotation, "How do I love thee? Let me count the ways . . . ," what would "the ways" be for you in your current relationship?

IF you had to be the mattress of one famous person, whose would you want to be?

IF you could add one phrase or statement to all marriage ceremonies, what would you add?

IF you wanted to nonverbally signal to your lover in public that you wanted a kiss, how would you do it?

Would you just pucker your lips toward your lover and glance sexily at him, or would you lightly kiss your fingertips, then blow it in his direction? Either way, he'd get the nonverbal message. Most couples in love are downright cuddly. More than 50 percent say they hug or kiss "anytime they have a chance," while 36 percent get affectionate at least three times a day.

'TILL I KISSED YOU

Are you and your mate typical? When couples were asked about their relationships, it was discovered that:

53%   tell their mates they love them once a day or more.
17%   tell each other weekly.
3%   tell each other once a month.
4%   rarely say "I love you," and sadly,
23%   never say the word "love" to their lover.

Also, for most couples, a big fight often ends in prolonged silence.

33%   say they don't talk to their mate for at least an hour after a blowup.
21%   stay quiet for a day or more.
19%   keep mum for about five minutes.
27%   never stop talking at all.

Up close and personal, couples:

45%   say they'd share each other's toothbrush without a second thought.
36%   would only share a toothbrush in an emergency.
19%   would never share their toothbrush with their mate.

About 85 percent of men and women now believe it is okay to kiss on the first date, provided they feel comfortable with the person they're dating.

There's stolen kisses, lingering kisses, sweet kisses, French kisses, butterfly kisses, all kinds of kisses that bond a relationship. Soft and reassuring as butterscotch, a kiss nourishes and warms the soul. And when it's over, it lingers on the lips and lives in memory.

Quick and fast or long and soft, a kiss is always still a kiss and carries with it a closeness of someone's inner thoughts and moods. Sexually, it's expressive, exciting, warming and leads to the hunger of passion.

The longest kiss listed in *The Guinness Book of World Records* lasted an amazing 417 hours. Perhaps that's why Mae West was quoted saying: "Too much of a good thing is wonderful." While you needn't set a world record, note that longer kisses are generally more erotic than shorter ones. If you can kiss for four or five minutes straight, you're doing better than 95 percent of other people. Surveys reveal that most people kiss for only a minute before breaking lip contact to get ready for another one.

The secret to erotic, loving kisses is to make each and every kiss feel like the first. If you recreate the desire, the thrill, and the pleasure of the very first time you kissed your mate, each time you pucker up, your kisses will always be sensual, pleasurable, exciting and inviting.

The decision to kiss for the first time is the most crucial in any love story. It changes the relationship of two people much more strongly than even the final surrender; because the first kiss already has within it a type of surrender.

"I think he's going to kiss me. I wonder how I breathe. It's much better not to think things through, I need to just do it. So I do . . . He kisses me . . . kisses me for a long time and I'm still able to breathe." Did those thoughts ever enter your head just before that inevitable first kiss or was it a sweet, stolen kiss and you never even had time to think?

Do you remember your first kiss?

Can remember	93%
Can't remember	7%

Not surprisingly, most people do remember their first kiss; whether it happened ten or 50 years ago, it seems to leave a permanent impression on all of us.

Ⓢ TUCK IN TRAFFIC: MASTER THE ART OF KISSING

A kiss is to lovemaking what a key is to a car. It ignites the motor, sets off that first spark for what you hope will be a long and wonderful jour-

ney. And, along the way, after the rest stops, a kiss is the key to restart the engines.

But if kissing is a key, remember it must ignite two engines—his and hers. This is where confusion begins. Her key may be soft, elegant lip brushes; his might be a big, slobbering, tongue-in-cheek affair. While he is off to the races, she's still in the garage with the engine flooded out.

Men of style kiss well; and with their partner's arousal always in mind. Here's the deal. For women, kissing is pleasure. For men, it's prelude. To her, the kiss (especially the first one or two) is a playful, intimate form of communication that's meant to say, "I like you, I like this, I'm pretty satisfied." That's why she approaches it gently, slowly, without all the heavy breathing and tongue whipping guys are likely to be hot for.

The best advise, according to William Cane, author of *The Art of Kissing*, is to pay attention to these cues. Let her lead. Take your time. Be patient. Enjoy it for what it is. At least initially, keep them brief, closed-mouthed, and soft on the lips. He states, "*If* things are going to accelerate, let them happen gradually. And, let *her* do the accelerating."

Once a couple has gone beyond the jitters of first kisses, it's time for exploring to begin. The key to kissing is technique, and the key to technique is variation. Cane suggests that a man continue to take things slowly, gradually, then begin to play around a little. Try long, sustained kisses, which women generally like, sometimes with your lips really locked on one another and other times with them barely touching. Alternate that with little, brief pecks on the lips. Moving along nicely, eh? *Men's Health* Magazine suggests the following:

Men's Five Basic Tips for Better Kissing

1. Alternate heavy kissing with light pecking, playfulness with arousal.

2. Keep variety in your kissing life; avoid the same old tricks in the same old order.

3. Sometimes kiss each other just for the sake of kissing.

4. Other parts of her body welcome your lips: forehead, ears, eyes, neck, cheeks, chests, elbows, hands, fingers, etc.

5. Kissing can include sucking and nibbling as well. Use your imagination, and don't hold back.

⬡R EAD HIS LIPS

Is he a good lover? His mouth will tell you all you need to know. The next time a handsome man smiles at you from across a crowded room, read his lips. They're almost more revealing than his eyes, definitely more so than his words.

Is he a tightwad or generous? Affectionate or self-centered? It's all in the mouth. At a party, just move around the room until you meet the right lips. The mouth reveals personality characteristics; it has everything to do with what we take in and give back to the world.

1. **Indentations at ends:** This is a sign of immaturity. This type of guy enjoys pulling silly pranks and often uses them to deflect serious discussions. He is usually a sweet and cheerful guy, but is a poor decision maker who normally succeeds later, rather than sooner in life. He commonly has very high expectations of his mate, and expects that you'll take care of his every need inside the bedroom. *(George Clooney, Drew Barrymore, Jamie Lee Curtis)*

2. **Wide mouth:** This is a person who usually likes to take charge. He's aggressive, ambitious, fearless and fast-moving. He likes to rule the roost and has definite ideas about what's permissible— he'll even tell you what to wear and what to eat. He's the boss in the bedroom, too. When, where and how are all under his direction—it's his show or no go. *(Antonio Banderas, Julia Roberts, Melanie Griffith, Dennis Rodman)*

3. **Small mouth:** This type is very secretive, controlled and repressed. The small-mouthed man is a master at small talk but is cautious in doling out his time, money and affection. He's wary of others, and loyal to only a trusted few. He's not very affectionate, and love is always on his terms. Warm, huggy sessions are not in his cards, so don't crowd him or touch him too much or he'll run. *(Bruce Willis, Celine Dion, Jerry Seinfeld, Michael Bolton)*

4. **Down-turned corners:** This person is usually a loner. Generous, sensitive and a brooder, he never forgets a hurt. He'll need constant reassurances of your love before he can trust and confide in you. He gives lovemaking his all, and a woman's pleasure is of great concern to him. Handle with care—this man's heart is easily broken. But, if you give it your all, you'll put this guy on top of the world. *(Sylvester Stallone, Susan Sarandon, Kenneth "Babyface" Edmonds, Robert DeNiro)*

5. **Thin upper, full lower:** A thin upper lip means discipline, a full lower lip means a zest for life. This man is sensuous and self-centered. Avoid fighting with him—he's smart, sarcastic and doesn't censor his words. He's a sensual adventurer who loves variety. You'll have to work hard at keeping this type of guy interested, because he bores easily, is impulsive and has wander-lust. *(Michael Douglas, Helen Hunt, Damon Wayans, Sharon Stone)*

6. **Rosebud mouth:** Women want to take care of this type of man because of his baby-like lips. This cutie-pie gets away with murder because nobody forces him to grow up. He's self-involved and has to know that he's number one. This kissable man needs lots of loving and fussing and needs to be reminded that he's the best lover you've ever had. He can be fun but moody, so be prepared to nurture him. *(Johnny Depp, Demi Moore, Spike Lee, Leonardo DiCaprio)*

7. **Well-balanced mouth:** This is the most desirable mouth. Lips of equal size which curve up at the corners and meet in a straight clear line, indicate a well-balanced, optimistic individual with varied interests. He's as excited by ideas as he is by the opposite sex. He's usually the lover of your dreams, willing to please and be pleased. You'll need a good mind as well as good looks to meet and keep these lips. *(John F. Kennedy, Jr., Halle Berry, Brad Pitt, Jennifer Lopez, Tyson Bedford)*

8. **Thin lips, big mouth:** A person with tight, thin lips is not into sharing. He likes to talk, but doesn't reveal much about himself. He's usually not a tender guy, he's self-involved, brash and can be very sarcastic. In love, he's a taker, not a giver. Don't expect deep conversations about love—those three little words will be heard rarely, if ever. He wants everything now and may overdo things. He loves to be the center of attention and may come across as

insensitive; temper tantrums are not uncommon. In romance, he needs to know that you're enjoying yourself, not for your sake, but for his. His sensual ego needs lots of priming and stroking. *(Jim Carrey, David Letterman, Cokie Roberts, Michael J. Fox)*

LIPSTICK ON YOUR COLLAR

During kissing, most men (67 percent) don't mind if a woman wears lipstick, and 8 percent actually like it when the lipstick is flavored. A minority of men (25 percent) don't enjoy kissing someone wearing lipstick, usually because of the smell or taste.

Men who don't mind lipstick, actually said:

> *"I don't mind, provided the lipstick tastes good."*

> *"Not at all. In fact, I like those lipsticks that have flavor to them."*

> *"I love it when a woman varies things—sometimes wearing no lipstick for a natural sisterly look can be supremely sexy, other times wearing a blood-red, naughty-girl color or switching to hot pink—they all drive me wild."*

> *"I love coming home from a date with lipstick stains on my shirt and face. It's so romantic, it makes me feel like I'm in a movie!"*

YOUR LIPSTICK PROFILE

Ladies, compare your lipstick slant; or guys, compare your girl's lipstick slant to those on the following pages to gain valuable insight about personality characteristics.

LIPSTICK/LOVEABILITY CHART _____

1. Slant keeps close to original slant and tip shape.
   - Abides by the rules
   - Great follower
   - Does not like too much attention
   - Likes a schedule
   - May occasionally color hair to attract attention
   - Falls in love anxiously

2. Rounded, smooth tip.
   - Considerate
   - Peacemaker
   - Procrastinator
   - Soft spoken
   - Makes others feel comfortable
   - Falls in love eagerly

3. Sharp-angled tip.
   - Forgetful
   - Opinionated
   - Emotional
   - Dislikes schedules
   - Spontaneous
   - Falls in love often

4. Sharp-angled, but curved.
   - Animated
   - Comical
   - Entertaining
   - Loves attention
   - Great motivator
   - Falls in love easily

5. Rounded tip to a point.
   - Courageous
   - Family-oriented
   - A "doer"
   - A leader and gives orders easily
   - Exaggerates sometimes
   - Stubborn over little things
   - Falls in love quickly

6. Flat top.
   - Direct
   - Independent
   - High morals
   - Loves challenges
   - Worries about appearance
   - Falls in love carefully

7. Flat top, concave.
   - Exciting
   - Intense
   - Analytical
   - Makes a great attorney
   - Disciplined
   - Falls in love infrequently

8. Sharp angles, both sides.
   - Spiritual
   - Persistent
   - Intellectual
   - Judgmental
   - Mysterious
   - Falls in love cautiously

S IGNED, SEALED, DELIVERED: I'M YOURS

The following romantic settings are often cited by men and women for getting them in the mood to kiss: taking a stroll through a park or along a quiet street, holding hands, romantic movies, music, intelligent open conversation, poetry, back rubs, fireworks, roses, dim lights, cuddling, physical closeness, candlelight and twilight. In addition, most men mentioned: the smell of good perfume, admiring kissable lips, seeing a woman in a sexy outfit, looking at the opposite sex and getting turned on, and flirting as preludes to a kiss.

LIP COLOR

Pigments applied to the lips have been used to enhance feminine beauty for at least 5,000 years. As with the application of other cosmetics, coloring the lips sends a nonverbal signal of sexual arousal which evokes a particularly strong reaction in men. Research indicates that bodily arousal in both men and women does lead to more blood flowing to the lips, making them redder. Coloring of the lips, thus, lends weight to the hypothesis that it mimics the increased coloring that occurs in the female genitals of a woman who is sensually aroused.

WET LIPS

Many lipsticks are glossy to make the lips appear constantly wet, as if just licked. Licking the lips, when done mysteriously sly, sends a clear unspoken message of attraction.

Also, the tasting of food and drink provides an acceptable excuse for licking lips and gives ample opportunity for sending arousing signals to a potential partner. The sensuality of many foods, the eating of food with hands and the later licking of the fingers, allows for a full display of sensual confidence and competence. When we use our mouths in this manner, we are practically advertising our talents and hinting at what might be in store for a potential lover.

For women who choose not to wear lipstick, and for men too, there are many products on the market to gloss the lips with moisture, including flavored balms that anoint the lips with seductive aromas and textures.

SWOLLEN LIPS

Whatever the shape of your lips, their volume increases when you become aroused. Blood causes them to engorge, increasing their sensitivity dramatically as if preparing them for kissing. A number of fashion models and actresses have their lips injected with silicone in order to send a nonverbal signal of permanent arousal.

MAKING OUT IN THE "RED LIGHT DISTRICT"

As we become attracted to someone, our lips and mouth become increasingly sensitive to touch and other stimulation. Therefore, a man or woman standing at a party eating a delicious snack will, without realizing it, take even bigger mouthfuls and chew faster as he or she becomes aroused. Also, when aroused, people will actually touch their mouths more, indicating that they may wish to speak to you and/or kiss you.

A kiss is one of the most intimate and sensual nonverbal sexual signals that we have. The way we kiss someone the first time may have a direct effect on whether the relationship continues. Kisses are wonderful things when done well. They have substance (we blow them at people as if they could feel them land on their cheeks and lips), and they have sound (we send kisses down telephone wires). Kisses have incredible power.

It is important to proceed through the various developmental stages of kissing in order to feel not only turned on, but at ease as intimacy develops. If you attempt to kiss someone full on the lips before he or she is ready, you may force him or her to retreat or turn awkwardly away, offering you a cheek at best.

Ideally then, the progression starts out as follows: first kiss gently on the lips, mouth closed; then slowly let the kisses become firmer with the mouth still closed. Next, part the lips slightly, as you feel the warmth of your co-kisser's breath. Since the lips and tongue are very sensitive to temperature, warmth is a sure signal of sexual arousal. Cold skin and lips are an indication to slow down and back off.

As passion increases we part our lips further, literally opening ourselves to each other. When "making out," male and female individual preferences vary greatly, therefore you shouldn't assume that someone likes to be kissed in the same way as you do. The strong, passionate kiss is a real turn-on for some people, but you should go gently and explore first. Your partner will show you, by example, how he or she likes being kissed if you allow the time for it. Tune your lips to your partner's and read what they're telling you.

If the eyes of a man or woman to whom you are attracted, meet yours, his or her lips will automatically part for a moment if the attraction is mutual. This movement is often very faint. At the extreme, a sensual mouth and sexy lips can literally take your breath away, make you lose control and cause you to cruise right through the "red light district!" Desirable, erotic lips *always* speak louder than words!

TO LOOK OR NOT TO LOOK

The question of whether lovers should kiss with their eyes open or closed is of fundamental importance. More than two-thirds of people surveyed concerning this, indicate that they prefer to keep their eyes closed while kissing, but don't mind if their partner keeps his or hers open. Only one in three people likes to kiss with eyes open. Perhaps that should be taken as a compliment, since one 24-year-old once stated, "I prefer kissing with my eyes open unless the girl isn't that pretty."

We needn't worry about our appearance during kissing, though, because if your partner kisses with his or her eyes open, everything will be out of focus. Because the brain interprets nearby faces as erotic, you'll actually appear sexier to your lover when you're mouth to mouth. Speed and closeness reduce your field of vision, cause confusion and dizziness, and make things jumble together. It's similar to driving too fast and getting too close to the automobile in front of you; it distorts your vision. Notice the diagram. So, sometimes open your eyes while you kiss and enjoy the fuzzy, dizzy thrill!

AN ETERNITY OF KISSES

Some people think that a kiss is something you do with your lips. But a kiss is really something you do to make you and someone else feel better. Anything you do that feels good can be a kiss.

Sometimes you use your toes to kiss; on a hot summer day, there's an ice cream kiss; you can use your little finger to kiss a hurt away; and sometimes a flying kiss is the best thing to do. You can kiss a sunset; you can kiss a girl's hand; angel kisses can be done anytime, anywhere; and if you want, you can even kiss God!

For a truly comprehensive analysis of kissing, we've got to make a brief detour into the realm of zoology. It's an unquestionable fact that animals kiss, too. Animals, though, kiss for a variety of reasons and in a number of different social contexts. Comparatively speaking, chimpanzee kisses are probably closest to human kisses, but many other species of animals also kiss. Horses kiss during courtship, dogs kiss during play, and fish will often swim around with their lips locked to another fish's lips for hours in an exhibition of kissing stamina that few humans can match. Throughout the animal kingdom, kisses express tender emotions as well as strong sexual desire. As for what's going on in the minds of those fish when they kiss, well, your guess is as good as mine.

No matter who does the kissing, the locking of lips is a special kind of touching. Whether your kiss conveys a message of caring and love, passion and excitement, or lust and impatience, to be potent, it must carry with it your whole attention. We've all been kissed by mates that did a very good job, but didn't give kissing their whole attention. No matter how hard they try, parts of their minds are on something else. They're either concerned about missing the last bus, worrying about jobs, money, their kissing technique, or wondering if someone will catch them. One woman says, "William doesn't have technique . . . but when he kisses you he isn't doing *anything* else. You're his whole universe . . . and the moment is eternal because he doesn't have any plans and isn't going anywhere; he's simply kissing you. It's overwhelming!"

At last count there were 1,001 ways to kiss. Some, but not all, have been named. Have you tried all of these that I've listed? Do you have others to add to the list?

- **Lip-Only Kiss:** When the only part of your bodies that touch are your lips.

- **French Kiss:** Lips touch, mouths open and both parties begin to explore each other with their tongues.

- **Nip Kiss:** When you add gentle, little nibbles on your lover's lower lip.

- **Cradling Kiss:** When you hold your lover's face in both hands while kissing.

- **Switch Kiss:** When you kiss your partner's upper lip while he or she kisses your lower lip.

- **Zorro Kiss:** Also known playfully as the "Dueling Tongues" kiss.

- **Ear Kiss:** Kiss the ear as if it were a mouth. *Smack, smack, smmmmmmak!* A word to the wise, for many women a kiss on the ear is about ten times more arousing than a kiss on the mouth.

- **Neck Kiss:** Place tender kisses in the hollow of the neck, which is the small cuplike depression that the chin touches when you bend your head all the way forward. Kissing the center back of the neck or playful love nips on the side of the neck send warm fuzzies all over. *Note:* To avoid hickey marks on the neck, massage the neck with your tongue, instead of biting or sucking it.

- **Awakening Kiss:** Kissing your partner's lips gently at first, and then increasing the pressure until she awakens.

- **Butterfly Kiss:** When you lightly brush your eyelashes against your partner's cheek, or any other body part.

- **Vacuum Kiss:** Sucking the air out of each other's mouth and then separating with a Pop! You've become mystically close and actually allowed someone to "take your breath away!"

- **Cordial Kiss:** Take a sip of your favorite drink, keep it in your mouth, then kiss your partner and share the liquid.

- **Humming Kiss:** Humming her favorite love song while kissing.

- **Smacking Kiss:** The lip-smacking sounds of kissing, considered the music of passion, can be fun to make and hear.

- **Sliding Kiss:** Sliding your mouth down your partner's arms, neck and/or shoulders and kiss along the way. So go ahead, *sliiiiiiiiiiide* all across his or her body and stop to put tiny kisses along the way. *Smmmooooooch!*

- **Wedding Kiss:** Plant one smack in the middle of the lips. Make it a long, deep, soulful kiss that expresses your feelings. Men, don't be afraid to lean her back, a la Scarlett O'Hara style, and make it last a long time; you want to give the well-paid photographers a chance to get a good shot.

- **Music Kiss:** Whether it's blues or rock on a walkman, jazz or classical on a stereo, or country music on a car radio, 95 percent of lovers reported that they enjoy listening to music while kissing. The music kiss can unleash emotions, make you feel romantic and sexy, and evoke moods you thought you'd never feel again.

How do you keep the music playing? Find your boyfriend, your girl-friend, your sweetheart, your soul mate, your honey, your sugar pie, your darling, and pucker up! When your lover gasps in delight and breaks off from a passionate embrace demanding that you admit where you learned to kiss like the gods of love themselves, simply smile to yourself, lick your lips, close your eyes and listen to the melody within you.

Kissing can create the right feeling. Like music, if it moves you, you feel good all over. Kissing enables couples to slowly fine-tune their bodies, listening for the different sounds, tentatively at first testing the chords, then gently plucking the strings until the soft humming becomes a duet. Passion and energy increase and a string ensemble is formed, brass horns join in, base drums beat like a heart on fire, and finally the full orchestra explodes in a symphony of cymbals and violins. Bodies get busy, the music keeps playing, and the two of you tango all night long.

MINIMUM DAILY REQUIREMENT: THREE KISSES

The Minimum Daily Requirement of affection for a healthy relationship is three doses per day. The "minimum" is defined as one kiss per dose, or its equivalent. Other equivalencies are:

↦ 3 hugs = 1 kiss

↦ 1 "I love you" = 1.5 kisses

↦ 1 greeting card (sentimental) = 1.25 kisses

↦ 1 greeting card (humorous) = 0.5 kiss

↦ 1 call from work (1-minute in duration minimum) = 1 kiss

↦ 1 "love note" = 1.3 kisses

Smooth Operator

He waltzes in almost an hour late and doesn't even bother to apologize. Whenever he passes a mirror he stops, flashes himself a sexy little smile and runs his fingers through his hair. He always seems to butt in when you're speaking, he can't take a joke and wants to be the center of attention at all times. And, on more than one occasion, he's said, "Relax she's just a friend"; or "Sorry, I must have left my wallet and credit cards at home"; or "Honestly, honey, it's just for the guys—none of the wives ever go to these conferences!"

LADIES, START YOUR ENGINES

If this sounds like your partner, the bad news is you're probably going out with a love cheat. These signals are just some of the classic signs of a smooth operator. People with particular personality traits are more likely to be unfaithful or to lie than others. Researchers have discovered some startling similarities between people who are prone to deceptive tactics, and it was found that, one of the key characteristics of a potential love cheat is an excessive preoccupation with his looks. These skilled operators tend to be very self-centered, never remember birthdays or anniversaries, arrive late for dates and meetings, carelessly runs up debts, and rarely say thank you. One weighty distinguishing feature of the love cheat's personality is his delight in seeing people squirm and feel uneasy. If he shows a complete lack of sympathy for sick or injured people or animals, he enjoys embarrassing people in public and he plays head games with you, you may have one very smooth operator on your hands. Ladies, start your engines and watch for those red flags and the ones that follow:

→ People are more apt to lie over the phone than they are in person.

→ More than 70% of liars would lie again.

→ Ten percent of lies are exaggerations, 60% are deceptions, and the rest are subtle lies, often ones of omission.

→ Women usually lie to make others feel better.

→ Men usually lie to build themselves up or to hide something.

→ Men lie more often than women.

→ Only one out of seven lies is discovered.

People often ask psychologists if they can read what people are thinking just by observing their body language and, in particular, whether they can tell if someone is lying. The answer is yes!! Body language, voice tones, sentence structure, and emotions all play a large role in deception and catching liars. With ample study of nonverbal communication and careful observation of potential liars, deceiving signs can be detected.

Humans aren't born knowing how to mask their feelings, but we learn quite early, perhaps as early as 12 months and certainly by the age of two, we're pretty good at it. We are usually brought up to think that lying is bad. Most of us are encouraged to develop a keen sense of right and wrong and to feel guilty if we avoid telling the truth. As a result of this guilty or offensive feeling, as with any strong emotion, we begin to feel uncomfortable. Conflicts and uneasy feelings that occur inside us tend to leak out, exhibiting themselves in our nonverbal behavior. The extent to which this leakage (gestures that do not match facial expressions or words) shows itself when we lie, the easier it is to catch a liar. The consequence of discovery and the seriousness of the deception does make a person anxious and sometimes this nervousness and apprehensiveness are apparent in his body language.

Western culture has this thing called a "white lie," white implying good or at least forgivable, whereby we evade guilt on the grounds that the lie is for the best. Our body language rarely gives us away if our mind has let us off the "guilt" hook. In other words, if we believe that the lie will not hurt anyone, then less guilt is felt and the lying gestures are harder to detect. As children we employ the pseudo-magical trick of crossing our fingers as we tell a lie, but as adults, even if we hide our crossed fingers behind our backs as we lie to avoid detection, some "leakage" of our true emotions will appear.

YOUR LIE DETECTION IQ

Let's determine if you're already a pro at detecting a liar or if you need to read further. Examine each of the following questions and decide if the answer should be true or false, using your own hunches and detection strategy. Who knows, you may already be an Inspector Clouseaux (That's my Cajun interpretation of the spelling for his name.) or Lieutenant Colombo!!

1. If the eyes are the mirror of the soul, they're a dead giveaway that he's lying if:
   a. he turns his head away and avoids eye contact.
   b. he shifts his eyes to the left, then tends to keep them to his upper right.
   c. he blinks a lot.
   d. he looks directly into your eyes.
   e. his pupils dilate.

2. If you listen to his voice, without tuning into the words, you'll be able to tell he's lying if:
   a. he talks louder and faster, speeding to get through.
   b. he stutters or hems and haws.
   c. he ends statements with upward inflections, as if asking a question.
   d. his voice is more high-pitched than usual or has a whiny tone.
   e. he continues to yawn unnecessarily.

3. His facial expression is the key to detecting his lie, if:
   a. he smiles too much.
   b. his smile is a little crooked.
   c. he wears a totally blank poker face.
   d. he smiles for too long a time.
   e. he smiles with his mouth but not his eyes.

4. If you watch him closely, his body language will tell all if:
   a. he shakes his head in a yes sign, but utters a no as he answers a question.

b. he plays with his watch or shuffles papers.

c. he rubs his hands together, scratches and constantly touches his body.

d. he shrugs his shoulders and sighs a lot.

e. he plucks pieces of lint from his jacket sleeve.

5. His attitude is the key to detection if:

a. he looks puzzled when he's asked a question.

b. he keeps smirking.

c. he overacts, is too animated, or protests too much.

d. he answers questions a tad too thoughtfully or too carefully.

e. he continuously clears his throat.

6. It's the things he can't control that give you the best cues, so you know he's lying when:

a. his pupils dilate.

b. his rate of breathing changes.

c. he keeps swallowing.

d. his face and palms are sweaty.

e. he blushes or gets red in the face and neck.

How do you think you scored? Read through this chapter, and the correct answers will jump out at you. To check your Detection IQ, though, the answers and explanations are at the end of this chapter.

The truth is, detecting lies through body language isn't nearly as easy as people think. Psychologists studying deception emphasize that there's no such thing as one gesture or facial expression that will always be a dead giveaway. There are many signs associated with deception and if two or more of them occur simultaneously, you should take it into consideration that a person may be lying to you.

People can become better lie detectors by paying careful attention to what psychologists call "micro" expressions in others. Micro expressions are those tiny signs made by a person's body that don't quite match what the person is saying. When the voice, words and facial expressions of someone seem disconnected and disjointed, genuine emotions are being hidden and masked. When you try to say or recall things too deliberately, you can't get the timing right. Your actions just don't match your words; you nod a yes, but utter a no—quite confusing, don't you think?

THESE FOOLISH GAMES ARE TEARING US APART

Assuming that people are scared as they lie (which is a big assumption), their automatic system will cause them to sweat more, particularly in the palms. Their palms sometimes begin to itch, they become more nervous, and then they begin to scratch the insides of their hands. Breathing becomes uneven, throat and lips become dry, and swallowing seems to increase in frequency. The frightened liar generally talks less, speaks more slowly than usual, and chooses his words with extreme care. Many speech errors, such as slips of the tongue and mispronunciations of words, occur possibly because of the mental effort required to keep his story consistent.

Paying close attention to expressions for what psychologists call "leakage" of telltale emotions, can increase your chances of sniffing out lies and liars in your everyday life. Studies show, for example, that the vocal cords are harder to control than the face, so when people are lying, their voice sometimes sounds higher or thinner than usual. Interpersonal communications experts have also concluded that when a person is lying, his extremities will be more difficult to control. Emotional leakage in the body at the extremities (excessive shuffling or scratching of the hands and feet), but not in the face, is a definite sign of masking true emotions.

There also is a definite difference between the story formation of a true story versus a fabricated story. Every story that has ever been told is made up of three basic parts. An introduction, the body of the story, followed by the conclusion. In a true story, equal time is spent in recounting the three parts, but the key notation here is that when a story is true, it is not usually retold in chronological order. The story teller skips around and may give a fact relating to the end of the tale, somewhere in the middle of the story, instead of at its correct placement in the story line.

In a fabricated tale, the story teller spends little time recounting the introduction and the summary of the story. Rather, he spends the majority of his story-telling time on the body of the story. The key component in a fabricated story is that the body of the story is retold too chronologically exact, too detailed. The story teller usually indicates exact time, including hour and minute, or he may try to give too much seemingly concrete information. Attempting to seem more credible, he may also use words outside his normal vocabulary, or he may literally protest too much, overcompensating with anger or language that sounds unusually forceful or theatrical.

Interestingly, most people do a worse job of lying if the person they're trying to mislead happens to be physically attractive. Paul Ekman, psychology professor at the University of California Medical School in San Francisco, and a leading authority on lie detection, speculates the reason for this, is that the would-be deceivers feel they have more at stake in convincing someone attractive than someone they feel is unattractive. His research did indicate, though, that good-looking people, even though they don't always make the best liars, seem better at getting away with a lie if the stakes are high. Rationally speaking, since attractive people are used to be looked at and at doing well in social situations, they tend to be more confident, and therefore, more convincing.

One important factor when evaluating someone's truthfulness is to consider how much we really want to be tricked or fooled. Although we may think we're more cynical than ever in this post-Watergate-read-my-lips-didn't-inhale-check's-in-the-mail society, polls consistently show that when it comes to friendships and relationships, Americans still value honesty more than just about anything else. In other words, it's only normal to want to believe what we're told, whether it's the slick promise of a high-pressure salesperson or those well-meaning lies that grease the social wheels and spare feelings, like "Wow, that's a *wonderful* haircut!" In everyday life, if we're being misled, it's probably because we want to be.

With liars, you will probably notice blushing, twirling of pens or other objects, and doodling. An avoidance of physical contact, as if in anticipation that the person being lied to might be able to feel the dishonesty seeping from the liar's body, is also evident during a fabricated recounting of an incident.

The inner conflict that takes place during a lie prompts a series of subtle but perceivable twitches, micro gestures, and facial movements that flash across the face in under a second. When we are being lied to, we notice these gestures, though we are not consciously aware that we have done so. People who are lying often exhibit minute nervous ticks in the muscles of their mouths, usually only from one side, and in their cheeks and eyelids. They may also blink faster too, their eyebrows may twitch—again usually on one side—and their shoulders may move slightly.

Someone who is lying will often fidget, drum their fingertips on a table, or entwine their fingers together. Their toes will usually flex inside shoes, and their feet, especially if they are hidden from view, may begin to tap agitatedly.

Most importantly, when lying we often seem to revert to our childhood habit of taking our hands to our mouths as soon as we've told a false statement. This response is similar to that of a child revealing a big secret. Once he realizes that he has blundered, he grasps at the invisible words as if they were still floating in the air, and tries to stuff them back into his mouth.

Since, as children, we tended to cover our mouths after we lied, today, when we lie, we tend to do the same action, only it is somewhat slowed. This slowing process allows our brain to interrupt the natural process, overriding it by diverting our hands to a site nearby—most often the edge of the nose, the eye or the ear. This delay may range from a couple of seconds to as much as a minute. People sometimes wipe the mouth with a downward palm gesture, as if to clean away the guilt that is induced by their conscience.

◣ CASANOVA: HOW TO RECOGNIZE A LIAR

Desmond Morris, internationally established author of books on both human and animal behavior, adds to our knowledge of lying gestures by stating, "Both when lying and when listening to someone that we believe to be lying, we tend to tug at our left ear."

It is a method of signifying to someone that "I do not believe my ears!" "I don't wish to hear this!" or "Wait until you hear this one!" When the hand is brought near the ear, it is an unconscious gesture used by adults when they wish to blot out the words they are hearing. It is a disguised version of the blatant "cover-the-ears" reaction to an unpleasant noise. The person doing this has a secret wish to block the ears, but politeness prevents him from actually doing it.

Deceit also occurs when someone rubs the eye or the skin near the eye. This action is used to justify the closing of the eyes, or provide an excuse for looking away, at a moment when there is some kind of deception taking place. The gesture is done when someone wants to urgently cut off visual contact with his companion's eyes. By gently rubbing the eye, it enables him to look away discreetly. This eye avoidance occurs either when the gesturer himself is lying or when his companion feels he is being lied to. In both instances, the action distracts and makes it possible for the gesturer to avoid the companion's gaze.

When the tip of the forefinger touches the skin just below the eyelid and pulls it downward, opening the eye more than usual, the gesturer transmits the message that he knows what's going on and that he is not being fooled. By doing this, he seems to be implying that his companion is lying and that he does not believe him, or to signify the old expression, "I don't have a wooden eye!" This gesture, too, occurs when the gesturer himself is lying or when his companion is doing so. In some countries, the eyelid pull is synonymous with the message of "Watch out!" "Keep your eyes peeled!" or "They're trying to pull the wool over your eyes."

The eyebrow cock, where one eyebrow is raised while the other remains in place, can also mean skepticism. It is a prime example of a contradictory signal—half aggressive, half scared—reflecting a puzzled mood, in which the gesturer has been surprised by something, but cannot quite believe that his shock is justified.

Years of research in nonverbal communication have revealed that left-hand gestures are associated with lying, while right-hand gestures are associated with honesty. This is not to indicate that our left-handed friends lie more than our right-handed friends. The only reason the left hand is used for the lying gestures is because from the beginning of time, the left hand has been associated with bad and right hand has been associated with good. It's always been that way. In some of our Middle Eastern countries, the left hand is considered so distasteful, it is not even allowed on the dinner table, it is strictly used for wiping purposes. Notice the gasoline gauge in your automobile, the safe or full indicator will always be on the right and the danger or lower level of the gasoline indicator will always be on the left. For that matter, as you travel your "freeway of love," notice traffic signals that go from left to right. The right side, which is usually green, is lit when it is safe to go. But if the steady red light on the left is beaming, you know immediately to come to a complete stop or you'll be breaking the law and may get a ticket.

Another reason our hands are drawn to our faces when we tell lies is because we are trying to use them to distract our listeners from the words we are saying. Our rings, watches or colorful fingernails dazzle outward toward our conversation partner. Thus, it is believed that if the listener's attention is diverted by his observation of jewelry or fingers, he only listens half-heartedly to what has just been spoken.

▲PPROACHING HEARTBREAK HOTEL: LIES AT FIRST SIGHT

Lies can also be spotted at first sight. Some people close their eyes as they lie in order to avoid the listener seeing deception in their "windows to the soul." Eyes tell inner truths. Bearing in mind the significance that eye contact differs from culture to culture, it is difficult to assume that because someone is not looking you in the eye, that they are withholding the whole truth or being downright dishonest.

A look of exasperation at not being believed is a strong indicator to help you spot emotional dishonesty. Look for mismatches in signals, where one signal comes from one emotion and another from elsewhere. A brilliant smile, with shaking hands, shows surface confidence but inner tension. Sad eyes combined with a sparkling smile are sure indicators that something is not being said; either she is frightened, angry or has a mixture of the two emotions.

Look out, too, when expressions of concern are accompanied by body movements away from the object of that concern, or when denials of interest are accompanied by movements towards the person in question. As in someone saying, "I care for you and I'll never leave you," and clearly recognizes that you're upset, yet still physically distances themselves from you and head towards an exit.

The nonverbal messages associated with lying are just as important in a love relationship as they are to law enforcement agencies. During questioning of a witness in the legal system, authorities who suspect someone is hiding information or lying, do so by observing specific behaviors. If these are helpful in the courtroom, think how useful they could be to you in your love life. Observe these warning signs of liars:

→ nose-touching while speaking

→ ear-pulling or rubbing while speaking

→ rubbing behind ear while speaking

→ eye-tugging while speaking

→ covering mouth while speaking

→ consistent avoidance of eye contact

→ incongruity of gestures

→ moving body away from questioner

→ sideways glances

→ peering over glasses

→ crossed arms and legs, with body leaning forward

→ pointing body and feet towards exit

→ squinting eyes

→ crossing fingers

→ smirking

→ plucking pieces of imaginary objects off their own clothing

→ yawning unnecessarily

→ wringing hands together

→ rubbing back of neck (considered self-beating)

→ throat-clearing

→ guarding body with an object (briefcase, book, jacket, etc.)

Time stalls, when recalling a story, give a potential liar suspicious time to gather thoughts and formulate a more believable tale. Some time stalls are:

→ cleaning glasses
→ pacing back and forth
→ bringing fingers to mouth
→ placing a pen or pencil to the mouth
→ scratching head
→ biting bottom lip
→ shifting eyes to the left and then up to the upper right
→ placing tongue to side of mouth
→ looking puzzled or concerned
→ looking as if in deep concentration while tapping fingers or feet

LOVE SHOULD HAVE BROUGHT YOU HOME LAST NIGHT

Let's play the lying game. Who tells what kinds of lies? As you read each lie listed below, guess which lies belong to women and which belong to men.

 ## MEN'S LIES, WOMEN' LIES

Man	Woman	The Lie
___	___	1. I'm 37 years old.
___	___	2. I've never truly completed the Boston Marathon, but I have run around the block a few times.
___	___	3. Hey, I was just 10 minutes late.
___	___	4. Look, let's stop pretending to be romantic. Let's just be friends.

_____ _____ 5. An anklet is the sexiest piece of jewelry a woman can wear.

_____ _____ 6. Let's just take our time. No pressure.

_____ _____ 7. Your eyes are the first things I noticed.

_____ _____ 8. Bring your roommate along to dinner.

_____ _____ 9. What I really want is to just talk and be friends.

_____ _____ 10. I have a meeting with my boss at 12:45.

_____ _____ 11. I have to call home to say goodnight to my four children.

_____ _____ 12. I live out of state; I'm going back tomorrow.

_____ _____ 13. Oh, it's no one important, let the answering machine pick it up.

_____ _____ 14. Let's take your car, mine is out of gas.

_____ _____ 15. Hey, I tried to call you today.

_____ _____ 16. This is great spaghetti.

_____ _____ 17. Let's just fly to Vegas tonight!

_____ _____ 18. I was planning to go grocery shopping tomorrow.

_____ _____ 19. Don't worry, I'll never leave you.

_____ _____ 20. Sure, me too, if it's not classical music, I just turn it off.

The correct answers are at the end of this chapter. Look at your own responses, though, and ask yourself what led you to think a particular lie belonged to a woman rather than to a man or vice versa? The manner in which you approached each of these lies and answered each one, is rooted on your own gender-based assumptions, personal set of experiences and expectations of the way men and women behave together. Whether you are right or wrong in your guesses, you can learn a lot about your own thinking and assumptions of gender differences.

YOUR CHEATING HEART

Men lie. Women lie. Neither sex has any corner on shadowing the truth. Data, though, does suggest that men tend to lie more and with more devastating consequences for the other sex. What is most noteworthy about lies, is that the differences and even the similarities between men's lies and women's lies are packed with information you can use to develop more satisfying relationships and avoid toxic ones.

In psychologist Dory Hollander's book, *101 Lies Men Tell Women And Why Women Believe Them*, when asked how she came up with such a list, (Were the lies chosen for being the most outrageous? The most harmful? The most frequent?) responded by saying, "Actually these and several other factors influenced which lies made the final cut." She said she wanted a list that accurately captured the deceit, manipulation, creativity, machismo, and everyday flavor that emerged from the interviews she conducted for the book. Most of the lies she listed have several variations and a sense of diversity. The first 35 lies on the list of 101, each represent a different category of lie most frequently mentioned by the men and women interviewed for the book.

How you use this list is up to you. Could be you'll find it good for a chuckle or a quick "aha" of recognition. Or, you may want to use this list to ask yourself and your friends which lies you've been told or have told yourself.

Lies come in many forms, and not all are excusable. Some are particularly mean-spirited, and some are habitual. Recognizing that, my hope is to help people who meet up with dangerous and outrageous liars to recognize the species, cut their losses early, and move on.

Whether male or female, the lied to or the liar, I'd like you to walk away with:

1. A greater awareness of the fact that men lie to women much more than most of us acknowledge.

2. The realization that you are not alone in being lied to or in lying.

3. An ability to analyze your own lies and your reactions to lies you've been told.

4. New strategies for coping with relationship lies, other than a typically female silent avoidance or a typically male defensive denial.

5. Added insight into your own behavior and that of the men or women in your life, which comes from a better understanding of how and why we lie.

How do we keep our faith in the goodness of people, respect our intuitions and our hunches, and defend ourselves against hurtful lies and liars *before* suffering damage? It's a serious challenge. To help prepare you, following is a list of the most common, most obvious, most ridiculous lies that have been told.

101 LIES (THE BEGINNING)

1. I'll call you.

2. I love you.

3. You're the only one.

4. I've never felt this way about anyone else.

5. I've got to work late at the office tonight.

6. That's the best sex I've ever had.

7. You've got the most beautiful eyes.

8. No, I'm not married.

9. Sorry, I must have left my wallet and credit cards at home.

10. You just have to believe me when I tell you nothing's wrong.

11. I'm ready to make a commitment.

12. Except for a beer or two, I never drink.

13. My wife and I haven't had sex in years.

14. We'll get married *as soon as I* . . . .

15. I'll be home in 20 minutes.

16. It's not that I don't care—I just have to spend more time with my kids.

17. I've been celibate since we broke up.

18. I could never lie to you.

19. I always use a condom.

20. I can help you get a great job in my company (field).

21. I haven't seen her since she and I broke up.

22. I haven't done drugs (smoked pot) since college.

23. The only sexual fantasies I have are about you.

24. No, I don't think your thighs (stomach, breasts, hips, etc.) are too big.

25. I'm too tired.

26. How could you think I'd be interested in her? She's your best friend.

27. It's you and me babe—we'll make love all over Europe.

28. I'd never do anything to hurt you.

29. I want to grow old with you.

30. Believe me, my wife and I live very separate lives.

31. I've never been in therapy.

32. How many times do I have to tell you I'm not seeing anyone else.

33. No, I never said that.

34. Relax, she's just a friend.

35. I guarantee you, I'm not the father.

36. And on, and on, and on, and on, and on.

BUT WHY WOULD HE LIE TO ME?

Why would someone you care about purposely lie to you? To *you*, who truly believes you would be just as happy with the truth. Although very few of us want to believe that we are gullible. When we care about someone, we usually want to trust him. And why shouldn't we?

When we do meet up with a liar, we are so caught up on trying to understand what makes the liar tick that we lose sight of everything else. Instead, we should be concerned with why we disregarded our own good sense, intuition, and past experiences and began to believe him. Three possibilities stand out as to why we behave this way.

First, we tend to believe a man's lies because we feel we've never given him a reason to lie to us. We think that it would just make absolutely no sense for him to lie, when the truth would have been just fine.

Second, we tend to have a major perceptual blind spot for lies we just would never dream of telling. There are some things we wouldn't even dream of lying about, so we feel, why should he? Women use their own standard of basic honesty as the benchmark for gauging a man's honesty. As one 39-year-old divorced woman noted, it never occurred to her that men would lie about their backgrounds or their jobs, because she had never lied to them about such things.

Third, some women believe that if men lie, there's probably a reason for it. Sometimes, we link a man's lying to a particular woman who perhaps mistreated him, rather than to a particular pattern in his behavior. And, since this woman knows she'll never treat him badly, she can let her guard down, and their relationship will be an exception or so she believes.

It's easy to see how destructive these approaches are. If you aren't expecting him to lie to you and then he does, it's far harder to detect. Then when you finally catch on to his deception, you may even look to yourself, not him, for the reason. The result? Self-doubt. He's off the hook, and you try harder—with him or the next and the next.

Most women who have been harmfully lied to assure themselves that it won't happen again and totally miss the obvious patterns that spring from the different agendas men and women pursue. Men and women are different, see the world in different ways, and have been socialized different. Boys and girls are brought up differently, each with unique sets of values and attitudes. These separate socialization processes are still not reason enough for one sex to be able to get away with lying much easier than the other sex can.

Don't misunderstand. I'm not stereotyping all men. There are many, many decent men who don't lie. My only reason for mentioning why women don't think it can happen to them, is to make women aware of our thinking patterns and never-ending self-doubt.

At the beginning of any new relationship, my suggestion is for each person to hit his own reset button and start fresh, but trust your intuition and always keep in mind any learned patterns of skepticism and suspicion that you've picked up along the way. It's a reasonable and adaptive strategy and could save much heartache.

HEARD IT THROUGH THE GRAPEVINE

When it comes to lying, don't bet on men having a corner on the market. We all lie at some time and often it feels so natural, so absolutely right, that it doesn't even seem to register that we are lying or that the truth might just do as nicely.

Research on lies that women tell, deal mainly with women not being able to say "no." For example, a woman has been approached for a date, and would actually want to decline, yet voices something different. The forefront of women's "no" lies are:

"Maybe sometime."	Means: no
"I've got a boyfriend."	Means: no
"I've been real busy lately."	Means: no
"I'll call you sometime."	Means: no
"I'm not dating at all right now."	Means: no
"You're really nice, but . . ."	Means: no
"Let's just be friends."	Means: no

LOVE DON'T LIVE HERE ANY MORE

How do we tell when a relationship is over? The signs of a partnership that has run its course are often very different from those of one that, though painful, is still alive. Even when the body language indicates constant irritation, when interactions erupt into daily fights and when break-ups are a regular part of life, involvement may still be there. One quote that comes to mind as I type this and has remained in the back of my head throughout my life reads: *"Relationships that don't end peacefully, don't end at all!!"*

A relationship that is truly over, however, where one partner or the other has emotionally withdrawn, has none of these traumas; if it has, they are one-sided in extreme. We can tell when we have reached this point if we feel almost no emotion at all. A sinking feeling in the stomach or a too-heavy relaxation in the muscles of the back, signal that our comfort zone now makes no response to the presence of this person.

Other tell-tale signals may be a failure to smile even slightly at the thought of our partner or the sound of his or her voice; a lack of any sexual feeling when we are touched; and a lack of any strong emotional signals—even anger, fear or grief—when we interact. If you no longer find your partner's body signals impressive; or if you find that his or her body smell and taste are disgusting to you, it's time to move on, drive like wild into the sunset and perform a Thelma and Louise. At this point, you're mentally out of the relationship.

When the end is in sight, couples usually have stopped matching each other with posture or gesture. When two people are no longer attracted to each other, they only occasionally make or seek eye contact; they usually have stopped completing each other's sentences and they even seem to keep an internal rather than an external focus when they're together. The partner who is most ready to end the relationship will appear respectful, but unresponsive; with a voice that is low, unaroused and lacking energy. He or she will show little emotion, but behave in a calm and carefully thought about way. It is almost as though the gestures are not entirely credible. One hand may be an exaggerated hold showing the effort he or she is putting into making it work, while the other hand is nestled in a pocket, making the complete gesture not convincing at all.

This is not to suggest that neither party does not have strong feelings. Leaving a partner is not an unemotional act, even when there is no passionate involvement left. We may be anxious or fearful, with unease in our comfort zones, or cold hands and feet. We may be sad that the relationship has failed, and so we feel the rush of adrenalin or are tearful and drained. These are emotions about the past or the future. In the present, real emotional disengagement means that the person or relationship in question has no emotional—and therefore no physical—charge for us any more.

How can you tell, then, that "love just doesn't live here any more?" One good way is to take some time to look at your own body language when you consider ending a relationship. Notice what happens to your body when you say, "It's over." If you can say it, feel calm about it, state it with assertiveness in your voice and believe that every part of your body is in agreement, then this means the time is right to end the relationship. You may not feel deliriously happy, but your body and emotions, if not your mind, have made the decision for you. If you hear your partner talking about ending the relationship while showing the nonverbal signals described above, then it just might be time to accept the inevitable.

It is possible to mistake signals, though, thinking that a relationship is over when, in fact, it may have simply reached a crisis point. If your response to hearing, "It's over," is to feel strong emotion, such as tears of regret around your eyes, anger churning in your stomach, mismatched feelings with movements of your body, or deep insight that the relationship can be improved, then you are still emotionally involved. Whether you stay or go is your choice, but the emotional link may be worth fighting for.

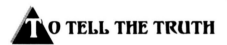 O TELL THE TRUTH

The solution lies inside each of us. The first rule of the road is to decide what you will and will not tolerate. People do lie, not just in the public world of profit, politics, business and sport, but in their private lives as well. We each have to defend ourselves, not the liar. It is time to take a stand. Don't deny your intuition, don't make excuses and don't fail to confront and hope for the best. Once you begin to reject your intuitive feelings concerning a suspected liar, the inconsistencies continue, and an endless cycle begins. The answer is self-defense. It's refusing to fall into the trap of positive thinking when your intuition is broadcasting that, truly, there is nothing to be positive about.

If we gave the same careful consideration and energy to making the truth as acceptable to the other person as the lie is, we would find that there are many ways to tell a difficult truth. A difficult truth is what is termed as a brutal truth. Truth is brutal when we wait too long to tell it, when we can't walk in the other person's shoes to understand his or her viewpoint, or when we lack skill in framing our truths in a caring way that the other person can hear. Truth is brutal when it is used as a last-ditch hit-and-run tactic—as in "I don't love you and I never did"—as he (or she) disappears into the night. If you must deliver one of these, consider the feelings of the receiver. If a brutal truth is worded correctly and delivered with sincere, honest, deep feeling, the pain is not as great. Take genuine care of other people; they're fighting battles, too!

By communicating our fear and discomfort in being honest, we find new strength and deep alliances where we anticipated rifts. Honesty strengthens our bonds with people. Even though the truth is rarely as glamorous or enticing as a well-told lie, when we and another human being open our hearts to each other, we also open ourselves to something of immense worth. In that type of connection, the *us* and *them*, disappears, and becomes *WE*. "We" is the first step to winning the lying game.

These three simple, but powerful, principles will help you move in the right direction. They should offer you some protection from the hurt feelings you get, when you're lied to or believe you've been taken advantage of.

1. **Respect:** Respect your own personal history as a source of wisdom; trust your feelings.

2. **Intuition:** Know that your intuition is a powerful insight that rarely misguides you.

3. **Boundaries:** Set well-defined boundaries as to what levels of truth and falsehood you will and will not tolerate in a relationship.

ANSWERS TO: YOUR LIE DETECTION IQ _____

How did you do? Let's examine each item for what the research shows to be true concerning lie detection.

1. The eyes do tell and questions (b), (c) and (e) are definitely true indicators of lying. If you selected (a) as a sure sign, you might want to think again. Some truth-tellers are so painfully shy that they can scarcely speak a word while looking you in the eye. Therefore, don't count on an averted gaze as proof of a lying heart. Smart liars know that everyone expects them to avoid their eyes while they lie, so they look you dead straight in the eye and tell you exactly what you want to hear. Give yourself a point if you did indicate that (d) is true, but be aware that this is not a foolproof method for catching a liar, since a truth-teller may look you in the eye too.

2. A person's voice does give clues of deception and truth. Seventy percent of people speak at a higher pitch when they are upset, tend to end statements with an upward inflection and want to hurry through the recounting of a story if they are extremely nervous. Therefore, if you answered true to items (a), (c) and (d), you're off to a good start. The problem is that none of this is that simple. Sometimes someone wants to recount a very detailed story step-by-step, consequently he chooses his words carefully and stops every so often to think through to his next words. Therefore, (b) could also be a true answer. One big sign of lying is unnecessary yawning. When someone needlessly brings his hand up to his mouth, it's usually done to divert the listener's attention from the facts of the story being told. Therefore, (e) is also true.

3. A genuine smile involves the entire face: mouth, eyes, forehead, laugh lines, and even teeth. Forced smiles, smiles that are too long, or smiles that do not involve the entire face are fake smiles, and are usually associated with masking. If you answered true to (a), (b), (d) and (e), you're on your way to being a great detective. How about a poker face? At its best, its purpose is to relay no information at all. Poker players wear their impassive masks to avoid giving away their hand. The poker face is more characteristic of introverted, analytical personality types than personable and silver-tongued liars. Usually it is the dedicated truth-tellers, not the liars, who wear wooden poker faces. The poker face is more likely an indication of a lie when it is markedly uncharacteristic for the person suspected of lying. Here, the message should be clear: establish what's usual for him before taking his poker face as a mark of a liar. Therefore, the answer to (c), can be true or false.

4. People who appear to be grooming themselves publicly by picking at their clothing, rubbing their hands together, or unnecessarily touching their bodies are more likely to be judged as liars. If you chose (b), (c) and (e) as true statements, then you're right on the money. Of course (a) is a sign of lying too; it sends out a mixed message from the spoken word. This should be your baseline, and any glaring discrepancy between what he says and what his body is doing may be reasonable evidence that he's at war with himself or isn't being honest. Shrugging shoulders is a sign that someone is trying to indicate, "Who me? Oh, I could never do anything like that." Sighing is an outright sign of agitation and occurs when

someone is disturbed concerning information being asked of him. Therefore, (d) is also true.

5. His attitude gives you a readout on three important factors. First, how fearful is he of getting caught? How much guilt or shame does he feel about lying? Is he having to prepare his answers before blurting them out? In number 5; (a), (b), (c), (d) and (e) should all be true answers. Puzzled looks are displayed to act as though he doesn't even know what you're talking about. Smirking and throat clearing are definite signs of nervousness. Unnecessary protesting, as in: "There is absolutely no way I could ever have committed such a . . ." is needless and pointless in declaring one's innocence. A dignified "yes" or "no" is all that is necessary when telling the truth. Someone who is hiding information is likely to pause five to six seconds before answering a question, rather than the usual, quick one- to two-second pause that is considered normal. It's what psychologists call "response latency." It's as if the liar is saying, "I'm thinking, I'm thinking," and buying time before coming up with an answer.

6. Now we're down to the wire. Autonomic reactions are pure, unacknowledged physiology: pupil dilation, patterns of breathing, sweating, frequency of swallowing, and blushing are all involuntary reactions that can't be easily controlled or inhibited by anyone. These are all good indicators of the lie. If you marked (a), (b), (c), (d) and (e) as true answers, you are on the road to becoming a super detective.

ANSWERS TO: MEN'S LIES, WOMEN'S LIES _____

The following lies were said by:

1. Female	8. Male	15. Male
2. Male	9. Male	16. Female
3. Female	10. Female	17. Male
4. Female	11. Female	18. Female
5. Male	12. Female	19. Male
6. Male	13. Male	20. Male
7. Male	14. Male	

7 Do That to Me One More Time

Rub me here, touch me there. Pull here, push there. Rhythmical movements of your partner's hands over your body creates a tantalizing, titillating rush of feelings and emotions. It feels great, it feels safe and you keep wanting to utter: "Ooooooh, it feels so good, do that to me one more time."

The flow, shape and softness of the naked female body has captivated artists—and mankind, for that matter—like no other vision. Nature, at its pinnacle of beauty, is the female body. From the sculptures of ancient Greece to the paintings of the Renaissance masters to the best of modern-day photography, there has been no better marker for style and grace than the shapely female body.

BEWARE: SOFT SHOULDERS AHEAD

The upper back, shoulders, neck and head all play a part in attraction. Everything from the angle and length of the neck to the texture of the hair affects perceived sexuality. Intimacy, trust and love are communicated by neck snuggles and shoulder rubs. The neck, ears, face and scalp are very sensitive and can provide unexpected erogenous zones. "Whisper in my ear and I'll follow you anywhere!"

Fashion allows women to have a considerable advantage over men in the upper back area, and a glimpse of a woman's back and shoulders through translucent material or peek-a-boo gaps in clothes can send fabulous sensual signals. Shoulders and backs are beautiful and have a language of their own.

The body statistics 36-24-36 will be familiar to many people, especially those who are faithful followers of the Miss USA or the Miss Universe pageants. The figures 55-38-07 are less well recognized, but they are perhaps of even greater significance. They refer to the proportions of the impact of a message or a touch in a face-to-face encounter. Nonverbal aspects make up 93 percent of a message, while only 7 percent of the impact is verbal.

Your posture, stance, mannerisms and even your curves reveal a great deal of information about your personality. A bared shoulder that is stroked or shrugged can be deliciously provocative. The curves and roundness of the shoulder area, particularly in women, are sensuous and arousing—as long as they are not slouching.

Hold your head up and people look at you; slouch and they look away. The posture and orientation of the head and shoulders speaks volumes about your attitude. The positioning of your upper body makes the difference between attraction and repulsion, either drawing people to you or pushing them away—something you may never have realized. Your head is capable of shaking, circling, tilting, waving or bobbing, and with your shoulders and head, you can weave and thrust, or shudder or shiver.

F EELS SO RIGHT

HEAD AND NECK

Touching implies that the actions are deliberate, conscious and primarily made by the hands. There's patting, stroking, shaking, kissing, licking, holding, guiding, punching and pinching. The type of touch used is dependent on which part of the body is touched, how long the touch lasts, how much pressure is used, whether there is movement after contact has been made, whether anyone other than the touchers is present at the situation in which the touching occurs and the relationship between the people involved. All in all, the determination for touching is a complex affair.

Touching can lead to liking, but not in isolation from other aspects of body language. You should not assume that if you go around touching people they will necessarily like it. Based on past experiences during childhood and young adulthood, attitudes towards touching vary considerably.

The old saying that, "The best way to knock a chip off a person's shoulder is to pat him or her on the back." Patting on the arm, shoulder or back can be a gesture of encouragement or support. Often, this is just what people with "chips" on their shoulders need.

Touching can often be used legitimately to attract attention, especially from someone whose attention is clearly elsewhere. It can also be used in guiding people to you or away from you.

Stroking and caressing, though, are touching behaviors reserved for those whose relationship is close. In intimate situations, these types of touches can occur on any part of the body: hair, face, head, hands, arms, shoulders, body, bottom, anywhere.

The head serves as host to the eyes, ears, nose, mouth, and brain; that is, the complete control and sensory functions for the application of nonverbal sensual signaling. The face is the principal asset upon which we are judged by others as being attractive or not, the principal stage upon which we act out our feelings and thoughts for others to see. The head is capable of numerous degrees of movement and angles, ranging from the tiniest, almost imperceptible to an exaggerated all-encompassing shake from side to side so that our chin touches our shoulders.

We use our heads to indicate direction, or signal to someone that we are interested in further contact. We turn our face towards them. We slightly nod at them. The smallest of our movements can be detected and can speak an entire sentence. If someone is talking with you, the more you respond to their speech with nods and words, the more they will be encouraged to continue talking, and the more they will enjoy being in your company.

Using head movements, we can determine whether the interest is mutual. The more relaxed and attractive the head movements, the more positive the answer will be. Since we tend to store tension, anxiety and stress around the neck and shoulders, a person with a stiff neck shows a lack of flexibility and is simply less sexy.

Early on in a verbal exchange, people tend to over-nod to show their enthusiasm for another person's company. Normally we nod in twos. If we nod three times in a row, it sends the message that we want to say something back.

The vulnerable and sensitive neck area is a more expressive part of our body than many of us realize. The sensual neck display appears in many forms. Women run their fingers through their hair and tilt their heads back to reveal the full extent of their necks. They will also angle their heads to one side to indicate that they're listening carefully to what someone is saying. This slight tilt is considered flirtatious and often arouses an admirer.

The muscles surrounding the spinal cord need to be relaxed and correctly positioned for us to be finely tuned and transmit positive and relaxed nonverbal communication gestures. Fear is capable of making the hairs on the back of the neck literally stand on end, but if on the other hand we find someone very attractive, our neck hairs will be soft and down-like, as we begin to experience a pleasurable tingling sensation throughout our body.

Women possess an excitable erogenous zone on their spine, six vertebrae down from the skull. It has been told of one woman who would wear her pony tail at just the right length to be able to tickle that particular spinal erogenous zone to experience pleasure throughout her busy day. To invite someone to rub your neck proves that you trust that person. The neck is one part of us that we normally reserve for our lovers alone.

While we frequently lean forward towards someone we feel drawn to, sexual interest is also apparent when the head is tilted back to reveal the neck and throat more openly. Both men and women do this, although men seem to respond more to the signal. The skin of the throat is often very soft and the rounded contours of the muscles mimic the more sensual areas of our bodies. It's worth noting that much of women's clothing today is designed to highlight or enhance neck length. Notice the degree to which deep, plunging necklines and stand-up collars emphasize and extend the neck.

EARS

Your ears have a vital role to play in seduction, so use them as much as you can. They will bring you plenty of information about the person you are listening to, both in terms of verbal and nonverbal language. Thirty-eight percent of our understanding of what people say depends on the sound of their voice, rather than on the words that they actually speak. We make many assumptions about a person from the tone, speed, breathiness and musicality of the voice—including how sexy the person is.

Ears also bring us information concerning our partner's breathing rate, thus enabling us to synchronize breathing patterns with them. The more in tune we are with another person, the more we copy their movements, including their breathing rate, speech patterns, mannerisms, and even their heartbeat. We tend to keep the beat of the same drum.

YOU PUT A MOVE ON MY HEART

When someone says, "I love you with all my heart," do they mean blood type, too? The Japanese believe that a lover's suitability can be determined by his or her blood type. Yes, you read that correctly. If you subscribe to this theory, I suggest that you go to blood banks to look for possible lovers. The four blood types are A, O, B, and AB. Here's what the Japanese believe each one signifies:

A   Represents "Eastern" values: Organized, follows the rules, scheduled—perhaps a bit too rigid. Most Japanese have blood type A.

O   Represents "American/Western" values: Creative, headstrong and callous, deciding one's own priorities.

B   Easygoing, carefree, sympathetic, kind.

AB   A combination of A and B: Organized but kind; scheduled but easy—a relaxed person.

Our own heartbeat reassures us that we are well. We dread its one day stopping, and we dread the heart-silence of those we love. Lying with your lover in bed in the morning, cuddling and dozing, pressed tight as two spoons, you feel his or her heartbeat and warmth enveloping you and sense a level of peace.

"How are you feeling, deep in your heart?" we ask. "My heart is broken," we answer, as if it were a block of chalk hit by a sledgehammer. Intellectually, we know that love, passion, and devotion do not lie in one organ. Yet when we speak of love, we use the robust metaphor of the heart, and everyone understands it. There is no need to explain.

Poems and music have traditionally been written in iambic pentameter, which sounds like this: ba-BUM, ba-BUM, ba-BUM, ba-BUM, ba-BUM. Of course, there are many other meters in which to write, but there's something innately satisfying about listening to a song or reading a poem written in iambs. It is a rhythm of a casual stroll. But it also locks up the heartbeat in a cage of words, and we, who respond so deeply to heart sounds, read the poem with our own pulse as a silent, private tempo. Music sounds and drum beats do put a move on your heart.

THE GENTLE FACE OF LOVE

A woman who is romantically attracted to a man will unconsciously tilt her face forward and to the side. This movement, combined with sideways eye glances, sends an intense sexual signal.

The actual proximity of our heads also speaks volumes. As we grow more intimate with someone, our desire to bring our faces closer together increases. The effect is two-fold: we exclude all other distraction from our field of vision and unconsciously prepare for our first kiss. As faces get closer together, by design our eyes can only focus clearly on one part of our partner's face at a time, therefore, we either see double or we keep our eyes closed. Why keep them open anyway? We don't need to see a thing at this point, and by closing our eyes we are better able to concentrate on the feel, smell and taste of the kiss.

Romantic attraction causes face changes. When a women is involved in a fresh, satisfying relationship, her skin appears softer and more youthful and her cheekbones seem to be more pronounced. This look is sometimes described as the "glow" of being in love. Arousal also brings a flush of color into a woman's cheeks and a high degree of romantic interest may produce a blush that appears on her neck, shoulders and chest.

Men touch their faces more often than normal when they catch sight of a woman whom they find attractive. They may stroke their cheeks up and down with the back of their fingers, touch their ears, rub their chins with their palm and pointer finger, and hold their head higher and more upright when they're aroused. Their eyes also appear to be brighter and more alive.

Women, too, stroke each part of their necks more, and touch their mouths and lips with their fingertips when they're with someone they're attracted to. They hold their heads up higher, their eyes shine and sparkle like a beacon on a clear night, thus making everyone near them aware that they're in emotional overload.

Our face muscles become more animated when we're with someone we're attracted to. We wink, we smile, we flush, we blow kisses, we cry, we scream; we yell passion with each and every expression.

HAIR

Let's talk hair: facial hair, head hair, hair coloring, hair style, hair length. Individual preferences concerning facial hair varies enormously. Some women love men with beards or mustaches; but most seem to regard clean-shaven men as sexier. Nowadays, though, designer stubble is regarded by some women as rugged and masculine and, therefore, attractive.

When it comes to hair length and color, research has revealed that dark-haired women are generally judged to be more serious, while dark-haired men are traditionally assumed to be more romantic than average. Women who wear very short hair are usually thought to be assertive and intense. Long hair on women is regarded as particularly feminine and alluring and can change the apparent shape of a woman's face.

Although there is no scientific evidence to support any of the hair color stereotypes, blondes are presumed to have more fun. Blonde women are often associated with sexuality and party-loving personalities, yet are judged less friendly and trustworthy. Blond men are taken less seriously and, like red-headed men, are probably believed less. People with red hair are stereotypically linked to possessing a fiery, tempestuous disposition. Wild, curly hair is thought to represent an artistic, cultured person who's quite unsettled and restless.

Nevertheless, we cling to the fantasy that very feminine women have long hair, even though we have all seen very attractive, highly sexual women with moderately short or even very short hair. Women with long hair do, however, use it as a powerful part of their nonverbal sexual repertoire, as do long-haired men. Those with long hair can toss back their heads in provocative preening gestures, and can even play peek-a-boo by peeking out from behind their hair like a curtain. They can run their fingers through it seductively, hide their shoulders with it, curl it sensuously around their fingers, and even put the ends of their hair into their mouths and gently suck.

Joan Juliet Buck, a devoted short-hair convert, has this to say in praise of women with cropped tops. "Hair is time. Women with short hair always look as if they have somewhere to go. Short hair takes a short time. Long hair takes a long time. Long hair moves easier than short hair because there's more of it. Long hair tells men you are all woman, or a real woman, or at the very least, a girl. Short hair makes them wonder."

Short hair makes children ask each other—usually at the school-yard gate, "Are you a boy or a girl?" I have found that once you've cut your hair short, you have to always remember to wear lipstick, but you can put away the brush, elastics, and the black rhinestone heart barrettes.

Girls with short hair, lose a nose and gain a neck, but a neck is generally better to have than a nose. It doesn't get in the way, it doesn't get the sniffles and it doesn't need to be powdered, but you begin to crave pearl necklaces, long earrings, and a variety of sunglasses.

Short hair removes obvious femininity and replaces it with style, it also makes you aware of subtraction as style. You can no longer wear puffed sleeves or ruffles; the neat is suddenly preferable to the fussy.

You can't hide behind short hair. Your nape is exposed. Men put their hands around your neck instead of stroking your long locks. You can only pray they have friendly intentions. The backs of your ears show, your jawline is clear to anyone watching and you may look a little androgynous, a little unfinished, a little bare. In fact, the first time you wear a bathing suit with short hair, you will feel exceptionally naked.

Short hair makes others think you have good bones, determination, an agenda and intelligence. The shape of your skull is commented on, so are its contents. People can pick you out in a crowd, and you can be recognized from behind, which can be good or bad. But, your face is no longer a flat screen surrounded by a curtain: the world sees you in three dimensions.

Hair preening, whether it's done with curly, long or cropped hair, will create sexual arousal. Men and women automatically touch their hair when they're attracted to someone; hair touching just makes you feel sexy. A woman who uses her hands to hold her hair, up on top of her head, while glancing sideways at her desired prey, is deadly!

LAY LADY LAY: THE SEXY UPPER TORSO

When we meet someone we like, not only do we give him or her a shoulder flash, we also give an eyebrow flash. Without realizing it, men and women slightly shrug their shoulders and lift their eyebrows when they find each other attractive. Each of these movements is small and rapid, but if you notice that the person facing you does it, you know they are attracted to you, perhaps even before they are aware of it themselves.

Have you ever observed what happens when a man and woman who are attracted to each other, walk towards each other? As the two approach, they both draw in their stomach muscles to make the muscles appear highly toned. As we pull in our gut to impress a romantic prospect, we puff up our chests. Women have the advantage of breasts, and can usually emphasize them with correct posture.

In correct posture, we hold our heads erect and maximize our height. Our faces take on a generally more youthful appearance. The bags and folds around the eyes are reduced, and the creases on the brow are smoothed. It is as if we are programmed to send the nonverbal signal, "I'm a potential mate for you and I'm fit, strong, healthy, and my muscles are toned up and primed. See for yourself."

Once two people have walked past each other, they tend to allow themselves to deflate rapidly back to their original posture. Someone with a well-balanced, upright posture, however, really stands out as special and attractive. Such a person has presence, and will be described as elegant, distinguished and even beautiful.

The condition and posture of our torso sends a clear subliminal message to interested parties about our readiness to reproduce. This may sound somewhat primitive, but it is, after all, what underlies all the complex rituals that surround nonverbal sexual communication.

Be body-aware. As you begin to converse with someone, turn your torso towards him or her. If he or she mirrors your movements, the stakes of the encounter are being raised. The closer you bring the central part of your body to his or hers, the more your intimate zone barriers will begin to merge. Each of us carries an invisible field of energy around us and it can be very exciting and arousing to bring two of these fields together.

PRIVATE DANCER

In romance, music is the food that's often used to stimulate passion and romantic involvement. It nourishes the mind, while exercising the body. Rushes of emotion and movement sweep through our bodies as we listen to the rhythmic beat of music. It's the magic love potion that changes our moods and conveys sentiments which are sometimes hard to put into words.

To be a skilled lover, it does require some degree of rhythm and animation. It is something we look for in prospective partners, and we can see it most obviously in the way a person moves their body while dancing.

In most cultures of the world, both music and dance are central components of courtship rituals. The sound of drum beats, while listening to a song, can change your internal rhythms: your metabolic and heart rates, your breathing and arousal level.

The melodies and harmonies of music cause movement and rushes of emotion to sweep through the body. Music is so powerful a medium of nonverbal communication that it can set the whole tone of an encounter: exciting and manic, classical and calm, soothing and New Age, romantic and sentimental. A shared liking of similar kinds of music often provides valuable common ground for potential lovers. Similar tastes provide a quick and enjoyable way of advancing to increased intimacy.

One very erotic dance or pre-dance movement a woman can make is to swing or gyrate her hips while standing still, with or without her hands on her hips. Armpits can be flashed while dancing with the hands raised in the air or touching the hair, providing a provocative sensual signal. The same is true of rolling shoulders and running one's hands over one's body.

Dancing is a dramatic way for us to put on a preening display for prospective mates. While dancing, we generally have full social permission to strut our stuff and it's an acceptable way of showing off our talents. Many dance movements involve the swaying of hips and torso and the stylized mimicking of sexual acts. The dance floor provides ample opportunity to observe body language of others. A person's dance style reflects his mood, shows how vividly and smoothly he responds to music and gives onlookers strong clues about his personality. Plus, body movements will certainly show if someone likes the music they're dancing to.

On the dance floor, mirroring and postural echoing can be employed to great effect. You can dance in synchrony with someone you've never even spoken to. Dance language will quickly tell you if your partner is attracted to you. If she or he begins to mirror your dance movements, this is a positive signal; conversely, if your dance partner changes movements every time you begin to mirror him or her, then take the hint and withdraw gracefully.

People not dancing, but wanting to do so, will indicate this with their bodies. Although they may be talking to others, they will move their hands or feet gently to the rhythm of the music, or sway their upper torso and shoulders in small dance movements. If you notice someone you'd like to dance with, and they're swaying their body to the beat of the music, more than likely they will accept.

Part of the dance routine will include the stroking of the waistline — especially in women, as this emphasizes the width of the hips and draws attention to the feminine body shape. Men also stroke their waistlines to emphasize the stomach muscles and to contrast this area with their wider shoulders and larger chest.

The slow dance is often the first opportunity we have to become really intimate with someone. How we respond while we're dancing close to someone tells us everything we need to know about our level and our partner's level of romantic readiness. Where we place our arms, how we move our bodies, how close together we bring our upper torsos, how much we allow our leg or knee to project between the legs of the other person, how tightly we hold each other, how much we relax into each other's arms, the amount of time we spend looking into each other's eyes, and whether our partner is looking over our shoulder can be observed to determine the degree of involvement felt between two people.

The angle of the torso (towards or away from a person) also sends a clear message of purpose. A full torso-to-torso position is quite common in slow, intimate dancing. It's a position where the entire length of the bodies are touching and it allows the partners to convey genuine feelings between the two of them. The hearts of the two dancers are about the same level; thus allowing feelings to easily flow from one heart to the other without much effort. If the partners are close enough, they can feel each other's heartbeat.

The male chest and the female breasts have both long been celebrated as central features of physical attraction and important tools in romantic nonverbal communication. The stroking, touching, fondling and caressing during the dance embrace produces strong sensual arousal and can very likely lead to romance.

Moving closer to someone gives you further information through both touch and smell. As we start to become romantically interested in another person, blood rushes to our skin causing our face, neck, chest, breasts and stomach to flush. The skin becomes far more sensitive than usual; we feel an emotional warmth, we tingle all over and we shiver with delight. Our heart rate rises, our breathing rate rises, our blood pressure rises—all biological responses preparing the body for action. The chase (as intense as a general moving his army without a map, or as gentle as voyeuristic pleasure) begins.

THE SCENT OF A WOMAN

Nuzzling can be surprisingly intimate and arousing because it's the natural aroma of your partner that's important. We like the way certain people smell and when we're near them, we have an unrelenting urge to rub against them and just sniff.

Ritual drums echo across the Canadian Arctic in the dusky mist as two lovers stand toe-to-toe and begin to rub noses in a prolonged Eskimo kiss. They rub noses, as well as smell each other. Although many men and women consider it childish on an intellectual level, more than 95 percent of people admit that they like to rub noses while kissing.

Each person has a unique, natural scent as individual as a fingerprint and probably there's nothing more exciting than the smell of your lover's hair or arms or neck; it's the strongest natural aphrodisiac, more powerful or potent than any perfume. Your scent has a lot to do with what makes you attractive and what attracts you to others. It affects everyone around you and can conjure up passionate memories of past loves and romantic, emotional encounters.

Certain smells we never forget. Mothers recognize the odor of their newborn children and babies can smell their mother entering a room, even if they can't see her. Mothers of school-age children can pick out T-shirts previously worn by their own child. This is not true for fathers, who do not recognize the smell of their infants, but can determine whether a T-shirt has been worn by a male or a female.

The keen nosed, Helen Keller, wrote, "My sense of smell has told me of a coming storm hours before there was any sign of it visible." She had a miraculous gift for deciphering the fragrant "layers" of life that most of us read as a blur. She recognized "an old-fashioned country house because it has several layers of odors, left by a succession of families, of plants, of perfumes and draperies." How someone blind and deaf from birth could understand so well the texture and appearance of life is still today, a great mystery.

She found that "masculine smells are, as a rule, stronger, more vivid, more widely differentiated than those of women." In the odor of young men she found something elemental, as of fire, storm, and sea. And, of them she noted, "They pulsate with buoyancy and desire and suggest all things strong, beautiful and joyous."

Some aromas last for a lifetime. Perfumes allow our scent to remain on pillows, on sheets or on towels long after we have gone. Fragrances can be floral, sweet, spicy or earthy and usually their names can suggest danger, love, romance, seduction or security. Doesn't that seem an odd thing to do? Not at all. Perfumes are made to shock, fascinate or disturb us with delight and we crave it beyond all reason, maybe, in part, out of a nostalgia for a time when we were created and deeply connected to nature.

Imagine your partner inhaling deeply as he nuzzles your neck and whispers that you smell delectable, delicious, sexy, and naughty. It gets you excited, doesn't it? It's pure ecstasy! If the body smell of another is right, romance might be in sight. Evidence suggests that our natural body scents vary depending on our level of sensual arousal, and these changes can be detected, usually subconsciously, by other people.

Temperature's rising, kissing and hugging, and holding you tight, let me hug you for the night, your aroma seems soooooooo right!!!

TOUCH ME IN THE MORNING

Soft shoulders. Dangerous curves. Stop on impact. Contact, that is. We need it, we can't live without it. We crave the loving touch and the gentle caress of a comforting hand.

It is believed that the ultimate expression of touch happens during the slow, sensual movements of body massage. Between two lovers, a rubdown becomes a seduction visited upon ten of thousands of nerve end-ings; a tender lovemaking experience encompassing the largest sexual organ on your body—the skin.

Massage is an enormous bridge to physical intimacy and a great method of learning your way around a partner's body. It also happens to ease tension, reduce stress, and cure headaches.

Becoming a good masseur or masseuse is a skilled profession, requir-ing plenty of experience in the field, a willingness to explore and be playful, and an understanding of the art. Oh yes, and oil. Lots of great, slippery, glistening oil.

While there's no single prescription for a good, sensuous massage, there are some techniques and style of handwork that the profession-als swear by. You probably use some of them already, but it never hurts to add a few more moves to your repertoire. Just remember that massage is an improvisational art and that you're free to pick and mix whatever techniques might be particularly appealing to the two of you.

First, though, let's lay some ground rules, some core requirements, if you will. If you're going to be a world-class lover and masseur, you need to know what experts know about creating the right atmosphere of sensual pleasure and relaxation. Here are some basic first steps.

GET LOOSE. Since so much massage revolves around creating a re-laxed mood, begin by cultivating that atmosphere. Dim the lights. Get some soft jazz on the stereo. Crack open a bottle of your favorite liq-uid refreshment. Make certain that your partner feels safe in your hands and is expecting your touch.

CHECK THE OIL. If there's an essential tool for a good massage, it must be the oil; make sure that you have an ample supply on hand. Not only is it highly sensual, but oil lubricates the skin and eliminates the painful friction that will inevitably occur if you try to give someone a dry rubdown. You can start with something as elementary as baby oil or you can make your own using pure oils like almond oil or coco-nut oil, or more exotic ones like avocado or lemon-scented sesame oil. Whatever you use, be sure to warm it by rubbing it between your hands.

CREATE THE RIGHT FEELING. Make sure that your room is pre-pared. Think of it as a theater, and set up a space that establishes a mood. Light the candles and use soft music to relax your partner. Make sure the massage surface (bed, floor, table) is warm—about 75 degrees;

cold surfaces will make your partner tense up. Keep your oils close at hand and have a large towel laid out.

THE OPENING. Have your partner lie on her stomach, hands at her side, with her head turned to one side. Kneel down facing her, with your knees on either side of the head. Drop some oil all the way down her back, on either side of her spine, and begin to massage it with both hands in big, circular motions, one after the other, each overlapping the track of the previous hand. Keep your hands flat and your fingers spread. This is a practical stroke, serving to spread the oil around the area you're about to rub as well as check for areas of muscle tension. You'll find your partner's tension areas because rigid muscles feel as though they contain knots.

KNEADING. After the initial stroking, you'll naturally want to start working the tension out of your partner's body by using deep, firm kneading strokes with both of your hands. Kneading is just what you think it is. You take a small bit of skin in your hands and push down while circling, the way you might knead bread dough, or Play-Doh, for that matter. This is a simple squeeze-release action, with the fingers on one hand squeezing while the fingers on your other hand are simultaneously releasing. It's great for the shoulders and the neck. Try it and you'll start to get into a rhythm.

STROKING. This is just as it sounds, lightly caressing the body. You wouldn't think it would have much effect, but a light touch can actually be more stimulating than deep kneading, especially on sensitive areas of the body or places where the bone is close to the skin. Stroking makes a nice counterpoint to kneading, so you should mix the two wherever you think it's appropriate.

FRICTION. When you spot a specific area that you want to work on—to loosen tension at a joint, to get at deep tissue, or to ease out a knot—you'll want to apply direct pressure in a very narrow area. You can do this using friction. Using the pad of your thumb, press down and move your thumb in a circular motion. This penetrates the tension and concentrates the massage. It's great for small concentrated areas, like the neck. To cover a wider area of tension, use the flat of your hand in the same manner in which you used the pad of your thumb. For fleshy areas, like the buttocks, make a fist and use your knuckles to apply direct pressure using circular motions. Be certain to ask for feedback from your partner to make sure you're not pushing too hard.

WRINGING. When you're working on arms or thighs, you can try "wringing." This entails placing both hands on one side of the thigh, then with your palms open, pull in one direction with one hand and the other direction with the other, all the while applying gentle pressure and a slight twisting motion. If it feels like you're wringing out a wet towel, you're doing it right. Work your way up and down the inner and outer thighs, then bend your partner's leg in an "L" position and do the same for the calves.

PULLING. Here's an easy technique that's always a favorite. It's simply called pulling, in massage lingo. What this entails is grasping your partner's natural handles—the feet, hands, and their accompanying appendages. Take the right wrist in your left hand, put your right hand on your partner's shoulder, and slowly pull the arm taut. Hold that pose, and then release it. Try this a couple of times, and then move on to the other arm. Next, try the ankles (your partner may need to hold on to something in order to get proper resistance), and after that, try pulling on the head. Serious—it's a human handle, too. Cup your partner's head in your open palms, lift it, then tug it ever so gently from side to side (never yank or jerk any of the handles).

IMPROVISING. Okay, now you're on your own. The rest of the evening is yours. Just remember two more things: First, keep in mind that you can always glide from one massage point to another and back again at any time. There's no need to follow a specific regimen so tightly that once you finish, say, massaging a thigh, you feel as though you can't return to it later. Second, once you have made contact with your partner's body to begin the massage, NEVER, NEVER lose physical contact with your partner. Always manage to have something touching, whether it's your elbow as you get more oil or your back as you reach for the towel. Once contact is made during massage, to lose touch with your partner's body would break the connection and the sensitivity you first created when you began to rub him or her the right way.

OUT-OF-WAY PLACES

Drivers, like lovers, at times must yield for others to get by so they won't get run over. Along highways throughout the world, specific traffic signals are placed to help drivers determine who gets the right-of-way; but along love's freeway, not much is written out. Successful relationships are made up of couples who've mastered the art of give-and-take.

Men usually don't stop at "yellow lights" and find it difficult to decipher if a woman's signaling a red or, for that matter, even a green light when it comes to romance. Men fly through flashing yellow lights; women come to a complete stop, even when they don't need to. The same is true in lovemaking, men jump in with no stops while women cruise along slowly, stopping along the way for caresses and warm, tender touches. Although most men would never dream of publicly admitting their hunger to be held, caressed, and massaged, it is as real for them as it is for women. In private, one of men's biggest complaints is that the women in their lives don't touch them enough, and they go about it all wrong when they try. Perhaps then, it's women who've been misreading the signals.

In an effort to bridge this touch communication gap, psychologist and sex therapist Peter A. Wish, Ph.D., author of *Don't Stop At Green Lights*, identifies six *secret* places (we all know the obvious ones), men want to be touched and explains, once and for all, how women can stake a claim in all of her partner's erogenous zones.

Zone 1: *His Face:* The face is an ideal place to start. There are more nerve endings coming and going from your brain to your lips, tongue, and other parts of your mouth than there are coming and going from your arms, hands, legs, and feet put together. Brush his face with your fingertips, rub his temples, stroke him behind the ears, and finish it off with a vigorous scalp massage. This gets him relaxed and ready, both physically and emotionally.

Zone 2: *His Chest:* Nothing makes a man feel more like Tarzan than having his partner rub her delicate little hands across his chest. Try raking your hands through his chest hair, caressing his nipples, kneading your palms against his pectoral muscles, and tracing imaginary lines from his neck to his navel. He'll love you for it and plead for more.

Zone 3: *His Hands and Feet:* The extremities can take a beating over the course of a day's work, and a lot of people report severe tension in their fingers and toes. If you sensually work on those areas of your man, you can destroy his anxiety and create a deep sense of relaxation for him. Men like a deep muscle massage in the arch of their feet; with it, they go from Stressed-Out Stud to Relaxed-Carefree Romeo just after a couple of minutes.

Zone 4: *The Underside of His Arms and Legs:* Guys like to feel as manly in the bedroom as they do in the garage. But romance is about vulnerability, even for men. That's why their soft spots, the smooth, relatively hairless insides of their arms and the backs of their legs—their tickle spots—are highly erotic. The skin there can be made to feel incredibly alive. Some guys enjoy being teased in areas that are not expressly sexual, but are often arousing in a sensual way. Straddling that line between caressing and tickling is cool, but it's possible to go too far. Under-the-arm touching is ticklish for most people, so you shouldn't overdo it. Experiment and tune in to the reaction you get in a particularly touchy zone.

Zone 5: *His Rear End:* We're talking about the buns here, buns of steel, of course. Many guys like having attention paid to their behinds, and touch in this area can be a source of intense, borderline-illicit pleasure.

Zone 6: *His Ego:* Not all of his sexy spots are physiological. In fact if you really want to touch a man, nothing works better than a vigorous ego massage. A man's pride isn't as fragile as the cliches say, but a little stroking goes a long way towards making him feel open to intimacy. "Make him feel like a man, like you really want him," says Dr. Wish.

Gentle, reassuring touching on his "right-of-way," "out-of-way," or "obvious" zones can only make him come back for more. Men also want to know that they're pleasing the woman who's pleasing them, says Dr. Wish. When he's doing a good job pleasing you, be certain to let him know. I promise, *he'll be touched!*

EAST-END BOYS AND WEST-END GIRLS

So maybe you aren't from Mars and your lover isn't from Venus, despite what those books say. Maybe the two of you are from Saturn and Pluto. Or East and West. Or Houston and Hollywood. Or First Street and Fifth Street. Just as couples originate from different areas of the universe; men and women's needs originate from emotional, physical, and psychological characteristics. A woman needs to feel emotionally close to make love. A man needs to make love to feel emotionally close. Men and women travel at different sexual speeds: while one's accelerating, the other's following the speed limit; and while one's urgently shifting gears, the other's staying in neutral.

What is it that's eternally sparking a man's hunger for romance? Don't try to count the ways. How can you count to infinity? His desire for love is kindled by a complex mix of internal chemistry and external triggers as subtle as a smile, the smell of a certain perfume or the mention of a song's lyrics. By touching another person's body or his own, by a thought, a meal, a dream, his desire for love gets triggered.

Just as the level of desire and romance varies between men and women, so does the amount of sensual appetite a person has at any given moment. That hunger can vary enormously day by day, year by year, and is caused by the level of testosterone in our bodies. Both men and women are revved up by their testosterone levels. The difference being that men have all eight of their cylinders pumped with this potent fuel, while women's motors get just a small amount. Testosterone and other hormones are the fuels that create your sex drive. Men may be able to accelerate at a faster pace, but women slowly, steadily and gently steam up their engines and cross the finish line with equal vigor.

WHERE THE BOYS ARE

You don't have to leave the city limits to meet good-looking men. In fact, there are tons right in your own town. Take the following crash course in guyography (men map reading), and find out where the boys are, what they're like and how to make your move, and if needed, how to make your exit.

Library

1. *What he's into:* Hours of serious studying in complete silence.

2. *Why that's cool:* Smart is sexy.

3. *Your opening line:* "Mind if I sit down? Those people in the reference section just won't be quiet."

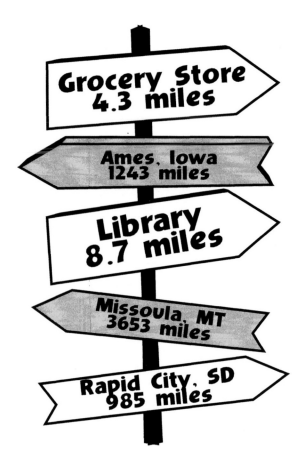

4. *Your escape route:* If he tries to impress you with his vast knowledge of the Dewey decimal system, plead the need for a photocopier and flee.

5. *If nothing else:* You've started some research on a topic that's interesting to you.

Record Store

1. *What he's into:* Two turntables and a microphone.

2. *Why that's cool:* He knows all the local bands, has great taste in music and actually likes to dance.

3. *Your opening line:* "Have you ever listened to this Quincy Jones CD?"

4. *Your escape route:* If you notice he has a Marilyn Manson CD in his hands, head straight to the check-out register.

5. *If nothing else:* He filled you in on the whereabouts of that hip, new dance club.

Coffeehouse

1. *What he's into:* Caffeine highs, long discussions and writing contemplative poetry.

2. *Why that's cool:* Caffeine is stimulating, and poetic men are deep.

3. *Your opening line:* "Do you have any Equal at your table?"

4. *Your escape route:* If his tattered journal is filled with funeral hymns and poetry concerning grief and mourning, recite spontaneous "Roses are red" ditties until he runs away screaming.

5. *If nothing else:* You've graduated from Sanka to espresso.

Hardware Store

1. *What he's into:* Building and repairing things with his own hands.

2. *Why that's cool:* He's willing to invest time and patience in worthwhile projects (i.e., relationships).

3. *Your opening line:* "I'm painting my dresser. What kind of paint do you think I should use—glossy or flat?"

4. *Your escape route:* If he takes off on a "tool tangent" and begins to talk about his sharp-edged saw, his two-pound hammer, his Phillips screw driver, or his power drill, tell him you plan to just use a stain, after all.

5. *If nothing else:* You've learned that stripping and sanding make for a smooth finish.

Baseball Park

1. *What he's into:* Getting a good workout and hanging out in the sunshine.

2. *Why that's cool:* If you strike out with him, there are eight others to choose from (and there's just something about a guy in baseball pants).

3. *Your opening line:* "Need a shortstop?"

4. *Your escape route:* If his desire to win makes him act like a jerk, pretend to have heatstroke and declare yourself out of the game.

5. *If nothing else:* You've proved that you don't "throw like a girl."

The Jogging Track

1. *What he's into:* Stretching his legs with his canine best friend, Amber.

2. *Why that's cool:* Cute dog, cuter guy—plus, walkers are easy to nonchalantly catch up with.

3. *Your opening line:* "What's your dog's name?"

4. *Your escape route:* If the conversation indicates that there are *two dogs* in front of you, fake an allergy attack.

5. *If nothing else:* You might run into someone else who's really great!

City Hall

1. *What he's into:* Saving this messed-up country, one protest at a time.

2. *Why that's cool:* He's passionate about his ideals and stands up for his convictions.

3. *Your opening line:* "It seems like you're fighting for a worthy cause. I'd love to help. Got a picket sign for me?"

4. *Your escape route:* If his passion leads him to handcuff himself to the mayor, offer to start a petition and hoof it on home.

5. *If nothing else*: You've raised your political IQ—and finally registered to vote.

Animal Hospital

1. *What he's into:* Volunteering to help heal pooches and kittens.

2. *Why that's cool:* With a heart that's so pure and selfless, he's got to be a sweetie.

3. *Your opening line:* "My cat ate my lace nightie!"

4. *Your escape route:* If he relates to Persian better than he does to you, ditch this volunteer and get a vet to help your pet.

5. *If nothing else:* You might snag free Eukanuba samples.

The Great Outdoors

1. *What he's into:* Biking, kayaking, climbing—if it happens outside, he's there.

2. *Why that's cool:* He'd be a great guide to take along on a hike.

3. *Your opening line:* "Your calf muscles look great."

4. *Your escape route:* If nature boy turns out to be a maladjusted loner, fake a spider sighting and make like Ms. Muffet.

5. *If nothing else:* You've picked up some wilderness survival skills.

House of Worship

1. *What he's into:* Faith, loyalty and devotion.

2. *Why that's cool:* He has morals and your parents and friends will love him—can you think of better qualities in a boyfriend?

3. *Your opening line:* "I'm thinking about joining the singles group. Do you know where they meet?"

4. *Your escape route:* If he reveals his belief that he's the Messiah, retreat to making cookies for the bake sale.

5. *If nothing else:* You've spent a little extra time reaffirming your beliefs.

Grocery Store

1. *What he's into*: Not going hungry and enjoying good food.

2. *Why that's cool*: He probably can cook.

3. *Your opening line*: "Is the whipping cream down this aisle?"

4. *Your escape route*: If he seems too anxious to show you, displays a distasteful smirk and you notice a Playboy magazine in his cart, make up an excuse to check on your three children in the next aisle.

5. *If nothing else*: You've completed your grocery shopping for the week.

Bus Stop

1. *What he's into:* A convenient, cheap and eco-friendly mode of transportation.

2. *Why that's cool:* He'll always have quarters.

3. *Your opening line:* "Did I miss the 3:30 to the mall?"

4. *Your escape route:* If he goes on and on in a monotonous tone about the intricacies of the bus timetable, crank up your Walkman until your bus arrives.

5. *If nothing else:* He's told you how to score a free transfer.

IT'S RAINING MEN

Men and women are everywhere, but there are more of them in large cities. This is simple logic. More people = more dateable people. Here's how the major cities, based on their male/female ratio of twenty-somethings, stack up. If you prefer older dates, go for the cities with the fewest twenty-somethings.

City	Number of men for every 100 women
Anchorage, AL	108
Austin, TX	107
Baltimore, MD	92
Boston, MA	99
Chicago, IL	99
Cleveland, OH	91
Columbus, OH	101
Dallas, TX	107
Detroit, MI	84
El Paso, TX	95
Jacksonville, FL	109
Honolulu, HI	106
Houston, TX	106
Indianapolis, IN	91
Los Angeles, CA	116
Memphis, TN	94
Milwaukee, WI	85
Nashville, TN	94
New York, NY	94
Philadelphia, PA	97

Phoenix, AZ	105
San Antonio, TX	98
San Diego, CA	124
San Francisco, CA	104
San Jose, CA	114
Seattle, WA	104
Washington, DC	90
U.S. Average	*102*

SMALL TOWN LOVER

Let's focus on the ladies for a moment. Just because a large city has men doesn't mean that they're your kind of men. The reason that California has so many men is that it has 100,000 prison inmates—the largest number of any state. Many of these guys are single, but they're usually not available for a night on the town. And in some cities—such as San Francisco—the men who aren't in prison are likely to be more interested in having dinner with each other than with a woman.

San Diego? Most of the men are in the service. Nashville? Many are struggling musicians waiting to be discovered. And unless you're a Gen X rep, stay out of Boston—too many college boys, not enough men.

Yes, there are more single people in large cities, but good things don't always come in big packages. Here are five smaller American cities that are great places to hunt for a man.

City	Number of men for every 100 women
Ames, IA	111.3
Rapid City, SD	98.7
Cheyenne, WY	97.2
Missoula, MT	96.8
Fargo, ND	95.7

EXTRA, EXTRA—WANTED: YOUNG MAN, SINGLE AND FREE; GOING TO PUT IT IN THE WANT ADS

A surprising number of people have met their mates through the personal ads. More than two million personal ads run each year. According to conservative estimates, more than 10,000 people a year who meet through the personal ads get married.

If you decide to place an ad, check the abbreviations to make certain you understand the lingo. Here are some of the most commonly used abbreviations:

S = Single	M = Male	F = Female	B = Black
D = Divorced	G = Gay	C = Christian	J = Jewish
W = White	A = Asian	N/S = Nonsmoker	P = Professional

Make your ad short and snappy. Don't lie, but make the most of your best!

Blue-eyed lady loves romance, music, tennis, dining. Seeking honest, good-looking lifetime buddy.

Me: Handsome, romantic executive. You: Educated, bright, very pretty, SBF, 29-35. As soul mates, we will find romance and adventure.

Funny, sexy, smart. SWF who likes to wear black hose, high heels and lace. Wanting male who's built like a brick house, is humorous and smart. Have couple will travel!! Call me!

She's Got Legs

Long, well-toned legs are considered very attractive in both men and women. The appeal seems to have less to do with the height than with the apparent length of the legs relative to the rest of the body. Good muscle tone is sexually attractive because it replicates the bodily changes that occur during a romantic encounter.

The legs have their own sexual language, and are particularly involved in the blocking and territory-marking aspects of seduction. Endless myths surround the sexual signals of legs. For example, many people think that crossing the legs is a defensive signal or a way of repressing sexuality. Sometimes this may be the case, but crossed-legs can send many other signals to interested onlookers too.

The leg-cross is the most potent, yet polite, sexual signal a woman can send with her legs and is a particularly attractive pose when viewed from front on. Generally a woman's legs are crossed in such a way as to appear highly toned with the length of the upper leg pressed against the lower leg and the uppermost foot often pointing towards the ground. Women, trying to gain the interest of a potential mate, will cross and uncross their legs in a calculated, seductive and deliberate manner to draw aesthetic attention to themselves. This classically feminine leg pose is less attractive when done by men. Women also have the ability to double twist their legs. This double twist is usually associated with being creative and talented, but is also a sign of feeling anxious and pent-up like a coiled spring.

FANCY LEGWORK

How you sit is a clue to your personality. There is a direct relationship between the way a woman sits and what's in her mind and her heart. Match the following postures given in numbers with the personality given in letters to determine how much you already know about legwork.

1. Knees together, legs parallel feet in line. _____

2. Cross legs at knees, with top leg slightly kicking up and down. _____

3. Knees together, toes together, heels apart. _____

4. One leg twisted around the other. _____

5. Knees together, feet wide apart. _____

6. Ankle of one foot resting on knee of other leg. _____

7. Feet together, knees spread apart. _____

8. Legs stretched out, one foot resting on the other.

_____

A. Scheming, thoughtful, and ambitious.

B. Shy, nervous, sensitive, frightened of life.

C. Self-centered, cold, difficult to get to know.

D. Confident, relaxed, forward, self-assured.

E. Imaginative, creative, artistic, talented.

F. Punctual, meticulous, loyal, well-groomed.

G. Unaware, practical, with little sense of self-consciousness, unsuspecting.

H. Athletic, masculine viewpoint.

Check your answers at the end of this chapter.

⬥DETOUR: BRICK HOUSE AHEAD

The legs and feet are central indicators of sexual attraction. We often forget to pay attention to our feet because they are at the periphery of our conscious attention span; we are so busy concentrating on facial expressions and hand and arm movements, but it's the feet and legs that can lead to information concerning another person's true feelings, emotions and sensitivities.

When seated, we tend to cross our legs towards a person we are attracted to, and away from someone to whom we wish to send a negative sexual signal. We point a crossed leg directly at someone we fancy, or in their general vicinity. Women will sit on one leg and let the other leg dangle to the floor, all the while pointing the bent knee towards their object of affection. We also point with our feet, and especially our toes, at someone who interests us.

There's pointing with feet while standing, too. We point a foot towards someone who attracts us, or move a leg in their direction. We can shift our weight onto the back leg, while keeping the other leg forward and bent at the knee. The female knee has a particularly erotic effect on some men; its roundness hinting at the shape of her breasts and buttocks.

If we really stretch a leg towards someone, it can be used as an invitation to follow it back to where it begins. Men tend to use the standard leg cross through habit and to dominate space. One way of signaling dominance is to "take possession" of a part of a room or furniture. Men dominate space and appear territorial, confident and masculine by leaning against a door post or wall, placing their hands on their hips, or spreading their legs in their chairs by putting one leg over one arm of the chair.

Men display confidence when they cross their ankles and place both feet on top of their desks. It's a very superior position and conveys a message of, "I think I'm better than you are." The cowpoke stance, where a man hooks one or both thumbs into his belt and points his fingers downward as if to frame his groin area, is an obvious courtship signal, and at the same time, allows him to display dominance and confidence. To appear sensual, while sitting, men will lightly stroke either their outer thigh or, less often, their inner thigh.

Both men and women do cross their legs at the ankle, but the message sent here should be interpreted in the context of accompanying signals—particularly how wide apart the legs are spread. Legs parted in a great yawning display send a crude, primitive sexual signal. Nevertheless, both men and women do automatically open their legs to varying degrees when in the presence of someone they find particularly attractive. It is more common for men to sit with their legs open, often giving a crotch display, although women wearing pants will sometimes also assume this position. Tight-fitting pants or leggings are highly provocative if they outline the shape of the woman's body through the material as well as emphasize the curves of her bottom. Men who wear tights for jogging or aerobic exercise also create quite a stir when the shape of their buttocks is exposed.

The cross-legged position, where one ankle is placed atop the knee of the other leg, is very inviting when used by either men or women. If the hand, though, is brought down to block the crossed leg at the ankle, it should be interpreted as a more defensive arrangement. Women use the leg cross to devastating effects and to play peek-a-boo with men. Skirts with splits allow women crossing their legs to flash tantalizing glimpses of that which is hidden under the material. Short skirts may be worn to deliberately reveal stocking tops or garters, which, of course, are considered to be highly provocative by most men.

Some dance styles incorporate courting rituals through the use of clothing to tantalize. For example, Spanish flamenco dancers wear the hem of their skirt looped around one of their wrists so they can lift and lower the skirt as they dance. Skirts used to their full leg-revealing potential, such as those made to rise up by swirling in a circle, can allow the sensually communicative women to coyly make her intentions known. Care to do the can-can?

◆ SEXUAL TRIANGLE: NO PASSING OR YIELD

Is your relationship a sexual triangle? Is someone moving in to disturb the balance of your connection between you and your lover? Triangular relationships—when one person is interested in two others at the same time—are often understood only through body talk. Secrecy so often rules in affairs that it is only through nonverbal communication that we really appreciate what is happening.

Imagine this scene. As three friends sit chatting, it becomes obvious what's going on. You watch as the man sits closer to his partner, who is seated at his right, but his body and gaze are directed entirely towards the "other woman" on his left who is sitting with them. He has eye contact with the woman on his left and his hand movement is clearly pointing in her direction. Meanwhile, she is confident of her effect. She leans back in her chair and angles her body towards him. She smiles warmly, runs her hands through her hair, then crosses her leg to face the gentleman. Her upper torso is open, and she reaches out for him across the table, pushing her glass well into his intimate space.

His partner begins to get wary. She now moves very close to him, away from the other woman, and well into his intimate space. She grabs hold of her partner's wrist in a restraining rather than a comforting way and her mouth attempts a smile, but it is not a genuine one. She feels anger and fear, but smugly tries to convey a confident relationship. Get the picture?

Whether all three people know each other, or whether only one person is linked with the other two, body language will alter as the triangle develops. The natural communication of intimacy between the original couple will change; new patterns of body talk will develop, both between the original couple and, if they ever meet, between the outsider and the other partner.

If you are an outsider moving into an already existing relationship, you will use all the body language of early attraction. Preening, displaying, eye contact; all these will be present, although, if under the watchful eye of a third party, they will be toned down—a touch under the table when no one is looking or a brief, intimate smile in passing. If anything, you will be less friendly to your potential lover than you would be if you were simply friends. If you are the potential lover, you will also be wary of showing too much, regardless of whether or not it was you who made the first move. You may be over-considerate to your partner, over-eager to be natural and unworried. But your mixed body talk will be obvious, your voice will be declaring no interest while your gestures will point clearly at your new object of desire.

If you sense an affair is possible, but want to steer clear, then you have the choice to signal this with classic "no" signs: closed posture, turned-away movements, little eye contact and, of course, no physical touch.

If you are an existing partner, watching your lover contemplating an affair, check first whether there is any real danger. Even overt flirting may be part of your partner's response to flattery, rather than a genuine attempt to have an affair. Check with whom he or she is matching body posture, verbal tone and especially, directional pointers. If the pointers are all towards you, relax; if they are towards a potential lover, beware. Then, consider what message you want to give to the outsider.

You will rarely want them to succeed, but if you're out with someone who is just a casual acquaintance and want to help him try to score, withdraw from your friend; show disinterest (not anger, which signals continued involvement), mismatch all your movements, lose eye contact and fail to listen when they talk. A potential intruder will be reassured and move in closer. If you want the outsider to back off, be subtle; defensive antagonism may provoke a rise to the challenge. To be really discreet, use all the body language of real friendship: move close; smile warmly, mirror your partner's movements, drop your voice to an intimacy level, invite confidences and, by all means, touch. The most obvious sign of possession of another person is to pick lint from his clothing. It gives a message of, "I chose this shirt for this person to wear, he/she's my partner." Even if there isn't any lint to pick, pretend there is and lightly brush his or her back with the back of your fingers. The message will speak out loud and clear. All these signals create enough of a bond between the two of you to let someone watching know there's a definite relationship going on.

TWELVE TERRIBLE SIGNS TO SUSPECT CHEATING

1. When he/she no longer wants to be intimate with you.

2. When he/she has a sudden change in work routine (leaves early for the office, has to work late, begins to have to attend many out-of-town meetings).

3. When he/she gets a whole new wardrobe of underwear.

4. When he/she begins to get mysterious phone calls, snatches the phone quickly after one ring, or the phone seems to constantly ring only once and then when you pick it up, there's no one on the other end. If he/she invests in all sorts of high-tech toys: cellular phone, private access code for checking messages, beeper, special beeper codes, etc.

5. When he/she arrives home smelling faintly of another woman/man.

6. When he/she arrives home and washes feverishly.

7. When he/she gets too nice too suddenly, or begins a disagreement for no apparent reason and uses it as an excuse to leave the house.

8. When he/she gets dressed up to go grocery shopping.

9. When he/she suddenly develops new eating habits, tastes or has an unexpected desire to tone up his/her body and begins to live at the gym, or wants a total new look and tries a drastic, new hair style.

10. When his/her excuses for being late begin to get too detailed, too elaborate and very complicated.

11. When you catch him/her in a lie at least three times.

12. Watch for a paper trail. If he/she doesn't let you see some of the monthly bills or suddenly has to get a post office box for business reasons. Oooooh, oooooh!

HOW TO FIND OUT FOR SURE

(From some who've caught the rascal.)

1. Smell him/her (and the car) for strange perfume or after shave lotion.

2. Get intimate with him/her soon after he/she gets home.

3. Follow up on any hints from friends.

4. If a working late story sounds fishy, create a sudden car/dog/ kid "emergency" so you need to reach him/her.

5. If you suspect he/she is dashing out to the corner store to make phone calls, follow discreetly to find out.

6. If you're quite sure, confront your mate immediately. Do not wait to catch your partner in the act and don't pretend you don't notice. The longer you wait, the longer your partner will keep messing around and thinking it's okay.

ROAD CLOSED: DO NOT ENTER

The standard leg-cross, where the right leg is rested over the left in a relaxed manner, can be used as a protective or closed position, depending on the context. This protective or closed stance is adopted when the leg-crosser feels threatened. When sitting in this manner the crotch area is hidden behind the shield of the upper thighs pressed together.

If legs are crossed defensively, this will usually be accompanied by a range of other defensive signals—the arms may well be folded, eye contact will be terse and abrupt rather than flirtatious, and a hand-bag or briefcase may be strategically placed on the lap, possibly as a large fig-leaf substitute. Further displaying defense, the torso will lean away from the accompanying person, or lean forward with the head supported by a shielding arm.

NO PASSING ZONE: DANGEROUS CURVES AHEAD

SEXY BUTTOCKS

The female curves can be emphasized by placing a hand on one or both hips and also by placing the body weight on one side while turning the torso at an angle to the man desired. Clothes that either hint at, or actually show the shape of, a woman's rear, sends shock waves of arousal through men. According to Harper's Index, the average increase in the protrusion of a woman's buttocks when she's wearing high heels is 25 percent. When a woman places her hand in the back pocket of a tight-fitting pair of jeans, the rounded shape of the buttocks is emphasized still further. Rubbing her hand over her hip outline has much the same arousing effect.

The more rounded and pert a woman's backside is, the stronger the sexual signal. A rounded backside is so important that researchers claim that the emphasis that many articles of clothing give to the breast cleavage is really intended to suggest the image of inflated buttocks associated with mating behavior. Women also visually assess the buttocks of men whenever the opportunity to do so presents itself. A small, tightly muscled behind is considered very, very sexy by most women.

SWINGING HIPS

Anatomical differences are responsible for the characteristic ways in which men and women walk. In women there is a greater rolling action of the pelvis, which causes more swinging of the hips. This hip-swinging walk sends powerful, erotic, sensual signals. The way a woman walks across a room can mean the difference between attracting a great deal of attention and being totally ignored.

When a woman touches her legs and thighs or strokes her knees, she sends yet another secret sexual signal. It is as though she is thinking, "I'd like to be touched here!" or better yet, "It would feel good if *you* touched me here!" Both men and women stroke their legs unconsciously when they are aroused, probably because the skin, at that time, is more sensitive to touch. As a man begins to feel increasingly attracted to a partner, he pushes his hips barely forward and stands with his feet slightly farther apart than normal. In this stance, one foot is usually pointing towards the woman he likes.

Either party, in this sex-oriented face-off, who wishes to exclude other people from their conversation, can extend a leg forward in order to build a barrier. If the other party meets him or her halfway in this maneuver with either foot or an intertwined leg slipped forward, the barrier becomes an intimate bridge that unites them both visually and physically.

This same type of barrier can be made when a couple is seated next to each other. Each will cross one leg over the other towards his intended mate, blocking all others out as if to say, "We are a couple, leave us alone." There are times when a couple who has become deeply interested in each other, will, in fact, begin to mirror each other's seating or standing positions. They will either both cross toward the left or

they will both cross toward the right. This high degree of synchronization in their body language suggests strong mutual attraction.

Shoes, and how we use them, say a great deal about us and often indicate our sexual mood. One of the strongest, deliberate and most obvious sensual messages sent by a woman is when she crosses one of
her legs towards the person she's attracted to and begins to slowly and
seductively kick her foot up and down in a "thrusting" motion. To show
further interest and intent, a woman might even slip her foot in and
out of her shoe or dangle the shoe from the tip of her toes provocatively. In fairy tales, shoes are often the vehicle of escape from humdrum lives. Therefore, when a woman seductively dangles her shoe towards an intended lover, it brings to mind the Cinderella effect of a girl
"almost" losing her slipper and then having it found and brought back
to her by a handsome prince who promises her a life of enchantment.

Anglo-Saxon wedding tradition requires that the father give the groom
one of his daughter's shoes to symbolize the transfer of authority. Also,
antiquated wedding custom demanded that shoes; not cans, buckets
or tires, be attached to the rear of automobiles used by the bridal
party.

One of the most astonishing sexual signals that a man can display to
show interest happens when he pulls up or adjusts his socks. It has
the same connotation as the woman's dangling of her shoe. Shoe styles
greatly affect men and women's sexual appeal. It also gives definite
clues to the wearer's personality and fashion style. There are enormous
individual differences in tastes and styles of shoes. Always put your
best foot forward and, *if the shoe fits, wear it.*

Length of leg is another arousal signal. Actual length is not as important as relative length: this is why slender legs are considered more
aesthetically pleasing, as they appear to be longer. High heels increase
leg length and are consequently considered sexy. Stuart Weitzman, a
leading designer of women's shoes says, "Nothing has been invented
yet that will do a better job than heels at making a good pair of legs
look great, or great ones look fabulous."

KILLER HEELS, SATIN SLIPPERS, SNEAKERS OR LOAFERS: YOUR SHOE IQ

1. The highest price ever paid at auction for a pair of shoes was $165,000. Who wore them?

   a. Marilyn Monroe

   b. Judy Garland

   c. John F. Kennedy

2. Where did women bind their feet to make them smaller?

   a. France

   b. China

   c. Sweden

3. Who invented our shoe-sizing system?

   a. Benjamin Franklin

   b. King Edward II

   c. Sir William Galoshes

4. How many pairs of shoes did Empress Josephine, Napoleon's first wife, have?

   a. 2 pairs

   b. 83 pairs

   c. 521 pairs

5. How many pairs did Imelda Marcos have?

   a. 522 pairs

   b. 783 pairs

   c. 1,060 pairs

6. Where did the oxford get its name?

   a. From shoes that resembled an ox

   b. From shoes worn by the Earl of Oxford

   c. From shoes worn at Oxford University in England

7. To "put your best foot forward," which foot should you use?

   a. Left foot

   b. Right foot

   c. Neither. This is a dumb saying.

8. When Lady Diana Spencer married Prince Charles, her size _____ shoes were decorated with?

   a. 8; sapphires and tiny, burning candles

   b. 10; white roses and diamonds

   c. 9½; pearls and mother-of-pearl sequins

9. Psychologists who have vigorously explored the hidden meaning of shoes from phallic symbols to secret vessels, claim that:

   a. Women who collect shoes are frustrated travelers.

   b. Women who can't get enough shoes are searching for enlightenment and knowledge.

   c. The average woman owns at least 30 pairs of shoes.

10. Childhood's classic slipper is the Mary Jane—the flat, blunt-toed, single-strapped shoe that confirms a child's transition from baby to little girl or boy, was:

    a. Named for a character in the "Buster Brown" comic strip.

    b. Seen on Marilyn Monroe in 1934 as she skipped across the screen in a white pair in *Baby Takes A Bow*.

    c. Worn by John Kennedy, Jr., as he saluted his father's passing casket in 1963.

11. Thigh-high boots were originally worn by pirates and smugglers, who tucked stolen valuables or "booty" into them—a practice that gave rise to the term:

    a. "One-legged bandits"

    b. "Bootlegging"

    c. "Booty Butt"

12. The term "barking dogs" is slang for:

    a. The wailing of back-yard dogs at war.

    b. The misnamed "wolf whistle" made by construction workers as a woman walks by.

    c. A person's aching feet.

13. Who said, "How tall am I? Honey, with hair, heels and attitude, I'm through this damned roof!"

    a. RuPaul

    b. Joan Rivers

    c. Naomi Campbell

A fresh start, a promise of romance and excitement—all little girls grow up believing the Cinderella myth that shoes can magically transform their lives. Shoes are a force for change, a means of shedding the past and buying into the future. For much of history women's shoes were kept in the dark, concealed beneath a froth of petticoats or a ballooning crinoline. While they were one of the most closeted parts of a woman's attire, ironically they are one of the most revealing items concerning a woman's character. Eyes may be the windows to the soul, but shoes are the gateway to the psyche.

Every woman worships the "right shoes," whether they're five-inch spikes or little ballet flats. The right shoes are different for every woman. You know them when you see them. They're the ones that start a pounding in your temples for no logical reason. They're the ones that make you tremble uncontrollably, though no one seems to notice. They're the ones that call you by your name in a voice that nobody else can even hear. The right shoes are the embodiment of desire. They represent everything you've ever wanted in your entire life, from that special doll when you were six to that date with the stud of your choice at 24.

Any woman devoted to her towering footwear, who's seemingly walking around smoothly and pivoting gracefully on her lethal-looking high heels, feels like a million dollars. And, when she's asked if her shoes hurt, she'll look you straight in the eye and say, "Oh, no. These shoes feel great." This, of course, is a bold-faced lie; but a noble one. The shoes hurt like hell; but if they make us look good, who cares! That's what is described as the shoe lover's eternal dilemma: the perfect pump in the wrong size.

Most of all, the right shoes are your best friends. Don't they tell you when an outfit doesn't go with them? Don't they give you confidence? If looks could kill, these shoes would be your ammunition. They have the power to transform you into someone you'd rather be—someone with the cool finesse of Ingrid Bergman, the style of Vanessa Williams, or the grace under pressure of Geraldine Ferraro. They allow you to step into an attitude, to assume an endless variety of identities, and still be yourself. Shoes do so much for you and ask only to be adored. How can you help but accommodate them?

Shoe shopping is the highest form of shopping as we know it. You don't even have to take off your clothes. Shopping for shoes satisfies the most powerful shopping compulsions with the least amount of effort and the most amount of pleasure. Nothing quite compares. You are catered to. You get to sit down and a salesperson brings them to you and slips them on your feet. Such luxury!

The feeling of being waited on during a shoe-shopping spree is the ultimate indulgence. It's so passive, yet so powerful. You can register disapproval with a wrinkling of your nose. "I don't think so," you can sneer, and the offending shoes disappear with the wave of your hand. You may ponder, calculate, coordinate, and agonize, all from your throne. All shopping should be like this. Life, in general, should be like this.

NOT DIAMONDS; HEELS ARE A GIRL'S BEST FRIEND

Having the right shoe for the right job is paramount to success. The following amusing shoe index will guarantee that you're well-equipped to deal with your everyday shoe requirements, as well as, your occasional shoe emergency needs.

POWER SHOES

POWER SHOES: Are an important asset to any woman's wardrobe. With them she can walk with greater confidence, climb to undreamed-of heights, and make others nervous. These can be a great tool of intimidation, in the most subliminal way.

BUSINESS SHOES: Find the most exquisitely designed (preferably expensive) simple black pumps you can. Remember, you don't want your feet to yawn "middle management." This aristocratically chic shoe, worn in the '60s by Jacqueline Kennedy, set the style in the White House. Every "First Feet" since, has adopted the pump as a hallmark of respectability and good taste.

DO-WITH-ME-WHAT-YOU-WILL SHOES: The most subtle thing about this naughty shoe worn by Jane Mansfield, is that your man thinks he's in control the whole time. Little does he know that you're calling *all* the shots—straight from your feet. This shoe is synonymous with the "come hither" look.

AUTHORITY SHOES: A good backup in case do-with-me-what-you-will shoes fail. Sure to scare the pants off Catholic boys. These tight-fitting buttoned shoes mold and hold a woman's foot, almost like laced corsets shaped a woman's torso! Ironically, the string or ribbon used to tightly lace the authority shoe has a titillating, pleasurable effect on men.

SHOES OF DEATH: Bad shoes for bad girls: definitely not on-the-job shoes, unless yours is a career in discipline!! Wear carefully. Those who wear these lethal-weapon shoes are thought to be aggressive, highly sexual, serious and must get the shoes registered with their local police. At least once in her life, a woman needs to don a pair of the "Shoes of Death." Be prepared.

💋 NON-POWER SHOES _____

For those occasions when you want to relinquish power or hide what you've got—or you just don't care anymore. Non-power shoes suggest a different, though still powerful, kind of magic. They are for those without serious intentions, who lack intensity and who like to play at love.

RHUMBA SHOES: Just right for those times when you want to dance the cha-cha, put bananas in your hair and feel compelled to scream "AIEEE!" Ruby red lips, a yellow-ruffled blouse and lots of curls on top of your head look tantalizing with these houchi-mama shoes.

PARTY SHOES: Imply a loose woman with a kind of devil-may-care fantasy. Everyone will mistake you for a reckless madcap heiress, giving you license to remove your clothes in public and splash nude in fountains, usually a refreshing change from your usual humdrum existence though, so go ahead and wear a pair!

MARABOU MULES: These are worn mostly as boudoir slippers and there's no other shoe that accessorizes a chaise lounge, a martini and a French maid like this one does. A must for those Mae Westian urges that come over all of us. The shoes which accentuated her hourglass figure added new dimension to her catch phrase, "Come up and see me sometime." Marilyn Monroe strutted her stuff in the marabou mule in *The Seven Year Itch*. The only way a man can respond to a woman dressed in this kind of shoe is either, "va-va-va voom" or "babyohbabyohbaby!"

DAISY DUCK SHOES: It's a fun shoe, a cartoon shoe that evokes a nearly lost world of innocence and simplicity. It should match an enormous bow in your hair and gives you an excuse to say things like, "Jeepers, what'll we do now?"

SHOE READING: FROM SOLE MAN TO TOE CLEAVAGE

The passions of true foot fetishists are in the hands of shoe designers. Some seasons, the uppers of shoes are high cut. Other seasons, they plunge low, revealing deep-toe cleavage. This gives foot fetishists a kind of thrill your basic "normal" person gets from ogling breast cleavage.

Sling-backs? This subtle device is a signal that otherwise "decent" women use to suggest that discipline is a factor in their lives extending beyond their careers. Open-toed shoes allow "respectable" women an opportunity to express their subconscious desire for lingerie featuring cut-outs in strategic locations.

Women, your little secrets are safe no more.

SHOES, SEX AND MEN

One look and a woman can tell everything about a man. Is he easygoing or straight-laced? Rich or poor? Messy or meticulous? Hip or conservative? The artistic type? Professional? Vice President or middle-management? From the Midwest or California? This is something that women are born with, an intuition they increasingly sharpen over the years. Faster than looking for that wedding-ring tan, more efficient than asking him what his sign is, more reliable than a computer dating service, it's called Shoe Reading.

Men think that when women gaze demurely downward, they're just being coy. What men don't know is that women are making a series of finely-developed observations that serve as a very reliable first impression meter.

WHAT HIS SHOES SAY ABOUT HIM

LOAFERS: Any would-be prepster who's too lazy to bend over to tie his shoes is in no position to take life by the horns. The key word here is "loaf." Tassels indicate even more whiffiness and indecisiveness.

SANDALS: If he's wearing the kind you can buy in health food stores, be careful. Next thing you know, he'll be telling you that you have beautiful energy that he'd like to explore. He'll want to know your sign and would love to observe the stars with you.

SUEDE DESERT BOOTS: Seedier intellectuals go for these. If your idea of romantic bliss is being at his place watching PBS documentaries on the Louvre and finding out that you've been sitting on a two-year-old deviled egg the whole time, go for it.

POINTY-TOED SHOES: Once worn by the kind of guy your mama warned you never to talk to, later a new-wave fashion statement. Now, again, worn by fellows nice girls avoid.

SNEAKERS: Could be a Bruce Springsteen-type who'd take you down to the river in his brother's Chevy and write a song about you if your name ended in "y," but more likely he'd lose his job at the gas station and ask you to buy all his auto parts for him or ask you out for ice cream on his tandem bike.

RUNNING SHOES: Usually he'll be wearing a pair of jogging shorts cut up to his zan-zan and he'll keep after you to race around the block with him. He wants the opportunity to see if your legs look more muscular than his.

COMBAT BOOTS: This rough'n ready blue-collar fellow can usually open his beer bottles with his teeth, loves to chow down on a big, juicy steak, has a good-cooking mama and wants a woman who will treat him like a cuddly teddy bear. He appears tough, but he's as gentle as a lamb.

WING-TIP SHOES: Usually wears a three-piece suit, carries a briefcase and is meticulous about the red, green, and blue pens he carries in his shirt pocket. He's precise in his wording, carries a tip card and would never leave more than the required amount of gratuity for service.

COWBOY BOOTS: Howdy partner! The guy in those tight, heavy starched Wranglers and western shirt is sure to be well mannered. He'll always open doors for you and will try his darndest to get you on his pony and have the two of you ride off together into the sunset. Happy trails, cowgirl!

KNOCK YOUR SOCKS OFF PLAYING FOOTSIE

Playing footsie is usually, but not always, reserved for people already in a relationship. It can be very exciting, particularly if it occurs out of sight (under a table, back seat of a car, etc.) and especially if it is performed secretively in the presence of others. What dinner table entertainment could be more arousing than to have your partner (or perhaps a new acquaintance with whom you have been exchanging signals of mutual attraction) touch your feet, ankles or toes, while above the table he or she remains apparently deep in conversation with someone else, seeming to ignore what is going on down under.

Feet contain some of the most powerful erogenous zones on the body. They're sensitive, wiggling things loaded with nerve endings. Because they're "down there" and sometimes considered dirty and foul, some unenlightened guys get grossed out. But, if you're a man who knows what a woman wants, you'll quickly learn that touching a woman's feet with a slow, masterful hand can have her squirming in seconds.

HOW TO GIVE GOOD FOOT

Scores of women and men agree that, when it comes to an explosively pleasurable sensory experience, a good foot rub ranks right up there with eating cake frosting from a can. If you want to be a lover who knows how to please, you'd better learn to give good foot. Here's how, according to Gordon Inkeles, author of *The New Sensual Massage*.

1. Take your partner's foot, begin kneading with your fingertips, and work your way from the ankle to the toes, all the while kneading both the inside and outside of the foot.

2. When you're through with that, push the tip of your thumb or all four knuckles into the depression of your partner's arch, again with gentle pleasure.

3. Same again, this time using your thumb or knuckle to put pressure on your partner's heel.

4. One by one, take each toe and give it a slow, delicate tug.

5. No tickling!!

FOOT FETISH: A WALK ON THE WILD SIDE

Some men and women desire or crave the presence of certain erotic elements to get into the mood for romance; the most common being feet. A foot fetish is a simple obsession by comparison to others. One man was quoted saying, "I love the female foot. When I see a shapely female foot encased in sexy high heels, I want to throw myself on the ground, begin worshipping her feet, and ask to suck each of her toes until I make her shiver!" Wow!

While the foot may be the object of his desire, it is not often the body part a woman considers her most erotic. Foot fetishists are advised to begin their adoration of their chosen female at a higher level and work down. Having one's toes sucked and instep licked can be a pleasantly sensual experience, especially if it's preceded by kissing and caressing the rest of the body. The man who dives straight for the feet will surely make his partner nervous. Certainly he wouldn't feel secure and comfortable either, if the "shoe were on the other foot!"

ANSWERS TO FANCY LEGWORK _____

1. F   2. A   3. B   4. E

5. C   6. H   7. G   8. D

ANSWERS TO KILLER HEELS, SATIN SLIPPERS, SNEAKERS OR LOAFERS: YOUR SHOE IQ _____

1. b, Judy Garland's ruby red slippers for her 1939 movie.

2. b, China. In the 10th century, according to social historians, exotic dancers at the Imperial Court wore tight socks to make their feet appear smaller. The custom spread throughout the upper classes and footbinding became a torturous procedure, as well as a rite of passage. A highborn mother would use astrology to determine the time and date of her daughter's *gin lien* initiation (to begin binding). This usually took place between the ages of 3 and 8. After giving the child a pedicure, she would bend the four toes back over the arch and bandage them in place. (The big toe was left free to form a half-moon shape.) After each bathing, the foot was bandaged tighter and then forced into a shoe one size smaller. The hope was to create a cultural rarity: a "Golden Lotus," or a foot measuring three inches. The only time the girl would see her feet uncovered from then on was when she was bathed or, after marriage, sometimes her husband would gently remove her shoes and unswathe the 10-foot-long strips of cotton or silk to use during their sexual foreplay. Chinese husbands respectfully coveted their wives' tiny Lotus

shoes and sometimes publicly display them on a small plate (with room to spare) to show off the foot size. Women commonly owned several hundred pairs and spent long hours embroidering them with symbols of fertility, longevity, harmony and union. Shoes worn on the wedding night often depicted explicit erotic scenes as a way of instructing the virgin bride. Openly practiced for a thousand years (Mao officially banned it in 1949), the foot-binding ritual is now a source of shame, and Lotus shoes have become collectible relics of a custom the Chinese are anxious to forget.

3. b, King Edward II. Men have been putting women on pedestals for centuries, at times verging on the ridiculous. In 16th century Venice, shoes called "chopines" placed women's feet on platforms that frequently rose to unprecedented heights of 30 inches or more. And we thought today's platforms were high! Made of cork or wood, the platforms themselves were usually upholstered in leather or jeweled velvet to match the shoes they supported. Venetian husbands reputedly introduced heavy wooden chopines to prevent their wives from straying. The chopine became a major symbol of social status, great wealth and usually two servants were required to steady the wearer of these impractical "walking footstools."

4. c, 521 pairs

5. c, 1,060 pairs

6. c, From shoes worn at Oxford University in England

7. b, Right foot

8. c, 9½, pearls and mother-of-pearl sequins

9. a, b, and c. The average woman does have 30 pairs of shoes, and psychologists have agreed that women who love shoes are frustrated travelers and are constantly searching for enlighten-ment and knowledge. Smart cookies!

10. a and c. The Mary Jane shoe was named for a character in the "Buster Brown" comic strip and John, Jr. did wear a black pair as he saluted his father's passing casket. Shirley Temple was the actress who wore a pair of these shoes in the family movie *Baby Takes A Bow.*

11. b, Of course, it's bootlegging, you didn't circle any of the others, did you?

12. c, Aching feet

13. a, No one else but the outrageous, outlandish RuPaul! You go girl!

Body and Soul

So, we've met, we're attracted to each other, we've spent some time together. We've kissed and we've touched. Do we want things to continue? You bet we do!

ROADMAP TO ROMANCE

Yield, one way, slow down, winding road, gradual curves, dip in the road, hazardous conditions, metered ramp, rough road, lane ends, crossover, maximum speed, U turn, wrong way, do not park, reserved parking, steep climb, do not enter, obey minimum speed limits, and be prepared to stop ahead. Sounds like traffic signals, doesn't it? The correlation between driving signals and relationship signs is amazing. Observe the similarities. By following, understanding and obeying the rules of the road, you can obtain a license to drive. Likewise, by having a consciousness for, and an awareness of, nonverbal sexual signals you can obtain a license to love. Your lover's license allows you to travel along life's relationship highways and tunnels without many detours or lane closures. And, just as accepting the responsibility of practicing safe and courteous driving habits are part of the process for obtaining a driver's license, it is hoped that they are also a prelude to securing a lover's license.

To legally drive, you must furnish:

1. your full name,

2. birth certificate or other proof of date and place of birth,

3. your physical description,

4. your home address,

5. a brief history of your mental condition,

6. your past driving experience, and

7. thumbprints.

To legally carry on a healthy relationship, similar requirements are necessary. If we are to interact candidly and sincerely with a possible lover, if we are to cautiously navigate with passengers in our lives and if our aim is to protect ourselves from harmful exchanges, we too proceed with caution and observe safety rules.

Whether it's to secure a lover's license or obtain a driver's license, tests are involved: there's a rules test, a signs test, a vision test and then the actual driving test. Your actual driving test will vary according to the type of driver's license you are applying for. Your lover's license will also vary according to the type of love relationship you're willing to become involved in. During the actual driving test, you are graded on your performance of some of the following actions:

→ parallel parking

→ quick stopping

→ backing

→ gear shifting

→ intersection observing

→ turning

→ parking

→ passing

→ following

→ posture (Keep both hands on the steering wheel and do not rest your elbow on the window.)

Imagine having a grading or rating scale for these actions in a love relationship. Would the scoring consist of simply pass or fail? Or should it read: A, B, C, and needs additional practice?

Upon completion of a driving test, a trooper/examiner will tell you of your errors and how to correct them. If you don't pass the test, you'll be told what items to practice on to improve your driving and when to return for another examination. Also, partners who are romantically involved will sometimes let each other know of specific areas in their relationship where improvements could be made.

If you do pass the test, you will pay the required fee and carry your pictured license with you when driving. If you're in an accident, you must show your license to any peace officer who asks to see it and to anyone with whom you are involved in an accident. Restrictions may be placed on your license to improve the safety of your driving and make you a better driver. In such cases a code letter is placed on your driver's license to designate your specific type of restriction or endorsement. Some driving restrictions seen on licenses follow:

A   With corrective lenses

C   Daytime only

E   No express driving

S   Outside mirror or hearing aid

T   Automatic transmission

W   Power steering

T   Double/triple trailer

H   Hazardous materials

Wouldn't it be great if people carried lover's licenses? Better yet, wouldn't it be helpful if a person's restriction or endorsement code letters were etched across his chest, and to get to know the person better, we'd just slightly unbutton his collar and peek inside? Using the equivalent driver's-license letters, what do you think human restrictions or endorsements might be? Could these work?

A   Likes peep shows

C   Night prowler

E   Ramrod kisser

S   Passive sex drive

T   Overactive hormones

W   Cybersex

T   Seduction addict

H   Halitosis

Lover's License

License to:
- ❤ Flirt playfully
- ❤ Be Passionate
- ❤ Kiss the Boys

Restrictions:
- ✗ Overactive Hormones
- ✗ Seduction Addict

Jane Doe-Eyes

"One is the loneliest number," sings the group, Three Dog Night; therefore, if you're tired of driving solo down life's highway, start scouting the horizon for sexual signposts. The key to successful courtship lies in recognizing the subtle signals people send out when they're attracted to each other.

H ANKY, PANKY

Restrictions, endorsements, ugh! Let's expand our minds and discover ways to use traffic restrictions and endorsements in a positive manner. Why not paint traffic signals on your lover's body. For example, a woman can paint words like "Speed Bump Ahead" on her partner's thigh, "Pedestrian Crossing" on his biceps or "You are here," almost anywhere. "Steep Hill" or "Dangerous Curves" are signs that can be painted in any number of places on a woman. Your body has many lanes, dips and parking spots. Have fun and *"paint the town red!"*

People who drive often develop relationships with their automobiles. They *love* them, they *hate* them, they *rub* them, they *admire* them, they carefully or recklessly *drive* them, and they *talk* to them. According to the book, *Everything Women Always Wanted to Know About Cars*, published by Doubleday, 45 percent of women talk to their cars, and some of their favorite sayings are: "She's such a good baby," "Hi cutie," "Bless you, sweet car," and "Damn it, start!"

While our minds, our bodies and the mechanics of steering are necessary for driving a car, a person's sex drive is determined by his or her obvious biological needs and certain specific psychological events. The human mind converts a scent, a sight, or even a sound, into sensual desire. Each person is triggered differently, based on preferences and attitudes that have accumulated since childhood. Some guys are fueled by legs, others by breasts; some women get acceleration from the sight of a man's shoulders, others by the sound of his voice. The little sparks that ignite our sexual engines are not just physiological; they're predominantly mental.

In fact, our minds are so powerful that in some cases, rambling thoughts overtake us. In the process of successfully stressing a point during a business meeting, a fleeting intimate memory of a past romantic encounter can rush through your mind and get you excited as well as aroused. Therefore, if you want to boost your rocket or put more tiger in your tank, light your fire by thinking sexy thoughts.

A IN'T NOTHING LIKE THE REAL THING: RULE OF FOUR

By now you've learned many of the individual traits of behavior that indicate whether sexual attraction is present or not. But just how sure can you be that someone is making a play for you? Is it just by chance that their body language seems to be saying, "I want you?"

The Rule of Four states: "To be sure that another person is communicating unequivocal nonverbal sexual interest in you, he or she must be displaying a minimum of four separate positive signals simultaneously, and these signals must be directed at you."

Keep in mind, though, that one of the complex games that people play is to flirt with everyone except the person in whom they are really interested. During attraction games, you may fall victim to being used as a mere pawn in an intrigue-filled chess game. It is also a basic human right for us to change our minds. Someone may come on to you strongly with four sexual signals, but the moment you start a verbal conversation with him, he changes his mind and his body language. Keep your eyes working in conjunction with your brain.

When you receive negative signals, no need to make a fool of yourself or make someone else feel awkward, just back off. Psychologists call these nonverbal negative signals de-courting signs. De-courting is most obvious through the withdrawal of attentiveness, increased use of defensive signs and a general reduction in rapport and compatibility.

Do remember that one positive signal can lead to two, three or ten signals in five minutes, an hour or even three months. There is no limit to the length of time that may elapse between the first minutes of meeting and eventual commitment to some form of relationship. Many signals of attraction may be seen in people who are just friends. Indeed, some of the best romantic relationships develop from friendships.

I 'LL SHOW YOU MINE, IF YOU SHOW ME YOURS

When first meeting people, it is as though we present a full-sized cardboard cut-out of ourselves, held at arm's length in front of us. On this board we display numerous trivial facts and figures about ourselves, our tastes in food and music, our work, our politics.

As time passes, we begin the vital work of self-disclosure. Inch by inch, we pull the cardboard cut-out to one side to reveal more about the "real" us. As with the "you scratch my back and I'll scratch yours," exchange, we do the same with information. The game is a familiar one; one we all played as children, called: "I'll show you mine, if you show me yours." This childish exercise served as one of the many developmental milestones we continue to rely on today, to understand nonverbal sexual communication. Adults continue to play the game, but with more intellectual information. Reveal too much too soon—like the stranger on the airplane who pours out dreadful personal problems to the unwilling, makeshift counselor—and the listener is put off. Reveal too little, especially when intimacies were revealed to you, and your listener will feel cheated and hurt. Keeping the scales balanced when revealing intimate information leads to building trust between two people, thus creating a healthier relationship.

Trust is central to successful seduction, sex and love. It is also vital for favorable nonverbal communication. Trust in your instincts, trust in your senses, trust your inner skills to understand and translate the sometimes elusive, near-invisible messages another person is sending you. If you detect reservation or doubt in your partner's face or body, respond.

The tiny subtle steps that our bodies go through as we grow more trusting of, and attracted to, someone else are deliciously exciting; each one deserves to be savored to the fullest, nurtured with care and enjoyed with pleasure. Each experience in building a relationship, especially in the early stages, is profoundly enhanced if we stay in the present, instead of dashing ahead or worrying over memories of earlier partnerships.

Assimilate all the messages that your five senses give you. Use your eyes with care; they are the principal tools with which to put into practice all the knowledge you've accumulated concerning sensual nonverbal communication. Scan the people you meet like a high-tech robot, noting every body position and the signals those bodies are sending out to others and to you. What are their eyes communicating to you? Eye-to-eye contact is one of the most intimate of all exchanges. Draw deeply on the information that other people's eyes reveal to you, and allow them to look into your mind in return.

Listen with care to all the sounds that people make; note breathing rate, listen for calmness in the voice, confidence in the tone and the animation and articulation of their speech. Take notice of the speed at which people speak and, most importantly, listen well to their words. Listening carefully to what someone says helps to find out who they really are, what they believe in, what they like and dislike and what makes them tick.

Every one of your senses will be of great importance to you in analyzing if it is to be an "all systems go" situation. Once you're involved in a relationship, get to know the smell and taste of your partner's body. Slow down and delight with your partner, enjoy the sensation of skin-on-skin touch; familiarity will be comforting, arousing, bonding and fun!

Experience passion with your partner by playing wholesome nonverbal sensual games. Using only body language movements, tell your partner how much you care for him. Think about it. Without words, how would you tell your lover, "I love you." Rely solely on the nonverbal signals of your hands, your eyes, your lips and your face—for that matter, your entire body. Let your body do the talking and play "show and tell." Get your partner in front of you, and by touching, rubbing and caressing, guess what your partner's nonverbal signals are for (1) "I like that!" (2) "I don't like that." (3) "I want to make love." (4) "I want physical contact, but no sex." (5) "I cherish you." (6) "I want to comfort you." (7) "I love you!" Ask your partner to confirm if your guesses are accurate. If not, find out from your partner what the correct signals are. If your partner doesn't have a signal for one of these seven messages, perhaps the two of you can come up with the appropriate body language gesture to convey the feeling. Go "parking" or practice "making-out" with your mate. Games like these give your relationship a kind of sexual "tune-up," and give you valuable insight to managing the switches which turn you both on. Couples who play together, stay together!

Romance has sometimes been labeled as "joyful togetherness." Not the type of togetherness where couples stay in close proximity to one another, but the togetherness of intimate sharing of time and experiences. Togetherness is about really connecting with your partner. Two people in love who are connected to each other can hold entire conversations without murmuring a word; the slightest touch by a gentle hand against an arm can speak volumes. A hand on a back, a small stroke of the leg or knee, the inquiring caress of a cheek, the massaging hand on the back of a stiff neck, a teasing touching of feet, a squirm-inducing tickle or a mischievous hand slipped into a pocket, all convey a language of their own. Touch between two people who are attracted to each other changes everything; it's a physical connection that's comforting and reassuring. In our adult lives we all have a need to connect for physical comfort. "Hug therapy," which consists of hugs, kisses and affectionate touches, can provide the healing, consolation and encouragement we each crave. Hug each other often, and hug well!

T HE STAGES OF NONVERBAL SEXUAL INTIMACY

While "checking out" someone we find attractive:

1. Eyes brighten

2. Skin around the eyes smoothes out

3. Muscles become toned

4. Body becomes more erect

5. Complexion reddens

When "approaching" someone we find attractive:

1. Body is positioned so as to be viewed in a positive fashion by the intended object of interest

2. Personal space is entered

3. Bodies lean toward each other, personal spaces merge

4. Facial expressions and body movements are highly animated and exaggerated

When "inviting" someone we find attractive:

1. Conscious preening

2. Increased self touching, leg massages, thigh supporting

3. Deliberate and intentional clothing adjustment

4. Twirling or playing with hair

5. Flirtatious glances, sexual peek-a-boo, full-body scans, gaze holding

6. Calculating eyebrow flash

7. Raised shoulder to expose rounded breasts (women)

8. Exposing the wrist and palm

9. Flashing genuine, natural smiles

10. Synchronization of body movements

11. Tilting slightly of the head

12. Moistening of lips

13. Slowly crossing and uncrossing of legs

14. Directional pointing of legs, knees, or toes

15. Playing with cylindrical objects (pens, pencils, glass stems, bottles, etc.)

16. Rolling of the pelvis (women)

17. Dominating territorial display of space (men) by leaning an arm or a hand against a door post or a wall so as to "take possession" of a part of the room

18. Calculating invasion of space with objects (pens, wine glasses, eye glasses, etc.)

19. Spreading legs in the cowpoke stance (men)

20. Pulling up socks (men)

21. Dangling shoes from feet (women)

22. Touching "accidentally"

23. Touching deliberately and seductively

24. Playful kissing

25. Intimate kissing

26. Softening of facial expressions

27. Tantalizing, titillating upper body touches

28. Stroking and rubbing of hips, thighs, legs and feet

29. Conversing through suggestive verbal invitations, flattery, confirmation

D ISTANT LOVER

We are dynamic creatures, perplexing of mind, skillful of limb, and vivacious of passion! Use your knowledge of nonverbal sexual signals to guide a person from flashing you mixed messages to confirming his or her interest or lack of it. You will know where you stand and what you stand to gain.

Begin by checking your own body language sexual signals. Perhaps you are sending mixed messages yourself and the prospect is mirroring you. Check your own motives: if you're about to play a game with someone, ask yourself why? Will any good come from it? Will anyone get hurt? Consider changing tactics in the list of this self-analysis.

If the person in question is leaning toward you and smiling, but scanning the room for someone else, he's probably being friendly while waiting for his date. If his arms are folded, but you're getting wonderful eye contact, a genuine smile, and his leg and foot are pointing in your direction, you may be the object of his desire. If you notice face touches, hair preening and sideways glances towards you, but his legs are crossed away from you and he's hand-in-hand with someone else, he's only flirting from a safe distance with you. He'd like to come closer but can't.

As with so many other areas of human behavior, we are daily confronted with contradiction and inconsistency in nonverbal communication. Few things are ever clear-cut. A woman might be very attracted to a man at first glance, but has to squash her natural inclinations and desires as she knows she is already committed elsewhere. Remembering the pain of ending a previous relationship, or a friend's warning about a new object of desire, can cause internal discord. We know better but we get involved anyway. Conflicting internal and external messages create the uncomfortable condition of simultaneous attraction towards and repulsion from the potential source of attraction or hurt.

While the mind knows better, at times the body reacts with an uneasy chemistry of physical desire. People often find themselves in the dilemma of thinking they don't find someone attractive, while simultaneously being undeniably drawn toward them. Complicated feelings and emotions will inevitably be communicated nonverbally. When words and actions don't match, it's just not the real thing. Mouths lie, bodies don't!

P ICK-UP LINES

Do you believe in love at first sight, or do I have to walk by you again?

So, is that a banana in your pocket or are you just happy to see me? Haven't you ever wondered where some people get their lines? So have I, and you won't believe some of the lines people have used or had used on them! My "scientifically conducted research," on pick-up lines, that I've gathered from friends, strangers, and those popular havens for pick-up artists, includes everything from the classics, to the creative, to the downright bold.

Although I don't guarantee that every line is for everybody, I do bet many will make you smile. Here goes. Learn a few. The next time you're admiring someone from afar and feel the urge, walk up, say something quirky and see what happens.

"I'll flip you. Heads—your place. Tails—my place."

"Hi, my name is Anita . . . Anita Man"

"I'm an army recruiter. Why don't you come over to my place and 'be all you can be.'"

"You da bomb!"

"Boxers or briefs?"

"Hello? Oh, your body was calling me from across the room."

"I bet your dad's a baker, 'cause baby, you got some great buns!"

"Do you like candy bars? Because I've got a Butterfinger that'll make you Snicker and scream . . . Oh, Henry!"

"Do you think I'm cute, or haven't you had enough to drink yet?"

"Miss December, right?"

"Hi, my name is Dick . . . Dick Fitzwell."

"Hi. I'm going to be a doctor."

"Do you believe in love at first sight, or do I have to walk by you again?"

"If your brain has as many curves as your body, you've got to be Einstein!"

"You look like my first husband . . . and I've never been married."

"Your body is like a gospel, and I'm shouting 'Lordy, Lordy!'"

"Care to dance the horizontal bop?"

"Do you mind if I sit down? When I saw you, I went weak in the knees."

"You must be one of 'America's Most Wanted' with a killer body like that!"

"Shh . . . can you hear that? It's my heart pounding for you."

"I've lost my phone number, can I borrow yours?"

"Screw me if I'm wrong, but is your name Zeldarita?"

"Excuse me, but where are your glass slippers?"

"Don't mind me, I'm just looking for your USDA prime grade beef stamp."

"Voulez-vous coucher avec moi ce soir?"

"What's your sign? Let me guess—Caution Dangerous Curves!"

B ARE YOUR SOUL: ASK FOR A PILLOW TALK

There comes a point where verbal communication must begin if an encounter is to move on to the next step. If you are unsure about the signals you've been receiving, now is the time to check them out. Begin a conversation with a possible partner and watch their body language. Verbal and nonverbal dialogue should smoothly interact; incidentally, when a person's verbal language contradicts what his body language is saying, give greater weight to the nonverbal signals. Bodies don't lie! If someone tells you they are not interested in a teasing and flirtatious manner, and continues to send you positive sexual signals, they may just be playing hard to get or trying to say "chase me."

Read the whole picture. The human body speaks from head to toe. It's unwise to focus on one or two very positive nonverbal sexual signals while overlooking many other accompanying negative ones. The combined message is the accurate message. Careful and sensitive assessment of the whole picture will ultimately help you to arrive at the correct interpretation.

According to *Men's Health* survey of *real* men, many guys are dying to please! "Tell us," they say. "Encourage us. We can't read your mind." Men are not clumsy and inconsiderate—they're just confused. Men say "We're more eager to please than women think." "We love romantic directions and feel that women who are verbal during lovemaking are exciting as lovers." Therefore: "Speak up ladies!"

You've got to admit that it does make sense. Women have long complained that men never stop for directions while driving cars, so why should they feel that men would ever ask for directions while making love. In romance, men don't mind back-seat drivers and feel that it's a woman's job to tell them when to stop, back-track, or take a detour. Whatever it takes to get to the final destination, in this case, they're willing to listen.

Women, it's said, talk a lot, but often hesitate to say what they really want when it comes to lovemaking. Women believe that a "lady" just doesn't do that. No one is born knowing how to give pleasure; therefore, there's really no alternative to speaking up. Some men need and want sensual direction and respect women who feel comfortable and confident enough to guide them through satisfying her. For once, this is where a back-seat driver does comes in handy. Literally.

One definite place for intimate conversations to take place, is on the couch during a pillow talk. Intimacy: we want it, we need it, we chase it, we fear it, and we run away from it. The price of intimacy is high; the price is yourself! Revealing your feelings through honest, heartfelt talks with another, creates inner peace within yourself.

For good pillow talk you'll need to:

1. light one candle,

2. get settled on the couch together early in the evening,

3. talk about your relationship—specifically what's working and what's not, and

4. understand that the purpose here is to connect emotionally with your partner—not hash out problems, deal with heavy issues or be sexual.

Sexuality is a language; it's one of the many languages humans communicate with. We constantly send little signals back and forth, verbal and nonverbal, consciously and subconsciously, as cues about our sexual state of mind, arousal, desire, and interest.

Most of us are hyper-tuned to these sex signals when we're first entering a relationship. We're all geared up to understand every sexual signal, but as the relationship progresses, misunderstanding and misinterpreting messages and cues—on all levels, not just sexual—begins. When any form of interpersonal communication deteriorates in an intimate relationship, lovemaking suffers. Developing good interpersonal communication skills in intimate relationships is vital to its survival.

SAY WHAT YOU MEAN. Mean what you say. Far too often we don't deal straight on with sensitive matters. If you want your partner to cuddle with you more, don't say, for instance, "You're not affectionate enough." Instead say, "I really like it when you lay your head on my shoulder and when you hug me and stroke me." It also doesn't hurt to add how it comforts you and makes you feel safe and secure.

ASK FOR WHAT YOU WANT. Many of us aren't very good at asking for what we want. We'd prefer that our partner just read our mind. You, better than anyone else, know what you need and want. Communicating your needs politely, positively, and encouragingly is key to a positive response. Mindreading is not *assuming* that you know what's on someone's mind; it's *knowing* what's on their mind. Can you develop mindreading skills? Of course you can. You don't have to be a psychic, you just have to:

1. listen carefully and pay attention,

2. respect what the other person is saying,

3. remember what was said during any discussion.

Misunderstandings cause grief and trouble in any relationship. Dr. Joyce Brothers once said: "My husband and I have never considered divorce . . . murder sometimes, but never divorce." From the ultimate best listed below, to the worst, how would you rate your relationship?

A relationship made in Heaven

Fantastic

Great

Good

Fair

Poor

Terrible

The relationship from Hell

BE OPEN-MINDED. An open mind is essential to developing, keeping and enhancing a healthy, loving connection between partners. It's the key to turning on your relationship's sexual engine if it has stalled. Ask questions. Assuming that you know everything about your partner's likes and dislikes is wrong. Become an open-minded, fascinated student of love and ask what may seem like the silliest, most basic questions. Routinely, practice pretending that your partner is a fascinating stranger you want to get to know better.

Jacob Bronowski quotes: "Einstein was a man who learned by asking immensely simple questions." Be an Einstein, try these with your partner:

1. If you're so smart, why aren't you a millionaire?

2. How are you just like your father? Your mother?

3. God wants an even dozen, instead of only Ten Commandments, what should the additional two commandments be?

4. If you could commit one crime with the absolute assurance that you would never be caught, what would it be?

5. If you were a member of the opposite sex, what would your name be?

LEARN THE LANGUAGE OF FEELINGS. Recognize what you are feeling and respond to that emotion. Relationships are based on feelings, not on facts. Learn, when you're upset, to say specifically how you feel to the person who has angered you, rather than call him names or hold resentments. No matter how tempting it is to attack, it will only harm the relationship. Venting frustrations positively will build, not destroy, closeness.

Idea: Practice makes perfect; make a habit of getting in touch with a variety of emotions. Each day this week, focus on one specific emotion with your partner for a few moments to test it out.

Sunday:	Tenderness
Monday:	Joy
Tuesday:	Peace
Wednesday:	Sadness
Thursday:	Kindness
Friday:	Passion
Saturday:	Love

TRUST. While tied to all the others, trust may be the biggest issue of all. You must be able to trust that your partner is committed to the relationship and won't suddenly run off with the butcher, the baker, and/or the candlestick maker. You must be able to trust that your partner will take responsibility for his or her own pleasure and will communicate to you when and what you can do to help. You must also be able to trust so that you can let your guard down with your partner and fully enjoy the relationship.

How do you repair broken trust? "With much difficulty," the experts say. The violation must be acknowledged openly and the hurt it caused must be recognized and communicated. There must be a sincere, heartfelt apology and there must be sincere forgiveness. There must be a vow that it will never, ever happen again. And, in every relationship, time must be allowed for the wound to truly heal. Expect that trust will be rebuilt slowly, one baby step at a time.

How do you increase trust? Start by sharing secrets. Partners need to feel completely confident that whatever is confided to each other will be respected and will remain confidential. In successful relationships, couples usually have secrets from the rest of the world, but feel free to share their deepest fears and insecurities with each other. The exchange of intimate feelings and the consciousness of sincere emotions between partners are the necessary ingredients for the creation of soul mates. The only realistic basis for a mature, intimate relationship is trust. You must trust your partner implicitly. Nothing else works.

M ORE THAN WORDS

Love. It makes the world go round. Money can't buy it. It's a many splendored thing. It will find a way. It will keep us together. Love. The most important concept in our lives yet we get haphazard training, conflicting messages and dysfunctional role models to guide us on our mission to find true love. What's a person to do? The answer is for each of us to know that love—like life—is a journey of self discovery. It's discovering your inner soul. It's delving deep inside your human spirit in search of your true values and beliefs. It's an investigation into what makes you happy, what brings joy into your life and also to determine how much pain you're willing to tolerate. You have to find your own way home. After all, there's no place like home, is there?

What do each of the following three phrases mean to you? Which of the three is easiest to express? Which is the deepest kind of love? Are you expressing all three in your current relationship?

1. Unconditional love

2. Physical love

3. Spiritual love

Writing helps you express yourself and explore your feelings. It allows you to focus your thoughts, dig deep inside your spirit to better understand your soul, and move you towards the joy and passion of love.

Relax, toss your watch aside, escape from the tyranny of the world of work and s t r e t c h your mind as we vacation in Sweetheart City, USA. Being on vacation is much more about a state of mind than it is about location—it should be natural, restful and easy. Our peaceful mini-vacation begins as we're coasting along the *Heartland Highway* through the *United States of Life.*

You won't need a seat belt, and you don't even have to own a driver's license. Poetic license, however, you do need to have. This trip, your own mental experience, takes you through the seeds of conception, the plains of adulthood, and the mountains of the middle ages. Understand that your mental vacation along the *Freeway of Love* will be rich with unexplored territory, gold mines, quicksand, rain forests, and ancient caves. You're free to travel at your own speed, take frequent rest stops and never pay any toll fees while on your pathway to inner peace.

On the journey, there'll be no red lights, green lights, or caution lights; only manifestations of mental, physical, and spiritual thoughts as you travel from one "state of attraction" to another. Upon your arrival at each state of attraction in your search for the intimate relationship, you'll find intersections marked by three major road signs: doubt, reassurance, and decision. They're signals to slow you down, to make you ponder about what to do next, and then to help you proceed accordingly in your search for truth and oneness. Growth. Fulfillment. Wholeness. Inner Peace. Flow. Centeredness. Literally and figuratively, physically and spiritually, love relationships are all about the struggles of oneness versus separateness.

The decisions you make at each intersection will bring you deeper and deeper into your heartland and put you in touch with the fact that you do have the power to control and rewrite your life, both on paper and off. There is a saying: "If you don't know where you're going, any road will take you there." Perhaps we're all tourists on the freeway of love, equipped with cameras for taking it all in, saving seashells, ticket stubs and matchboxes and wearing comfortable shoes for walking through life with a minimum of pain. The choice to slow down, to honor the flowers, to honor ourselves and other people, is ours. Experience every part of your journey, that is, take an active part in living. Vacations remind us of the importance of the Now. The more you live in the Now, the more vital you'll be, the more alive you'll feel, the more energy you'll have and the more romantic you'll become.

We are drawn naturally towards things that promote oneness. We desire connection and spend our entire lives looking for it. It's the place where the feeling of true belonging exists. It's called home; not the physical structure of a house, but the place inside each of us that houses our soul. Home is where the heart is! How often have we wished we could turn back the hands of time or said to ourselves, "If I had it to do all over again?" What if we could relive the precious moments of love in our lives and erase the memories that have left us scarred? There is a way; it's through the written word. Words are powerful and are some of the best vehicles to move us to true forgiveness of others. Unexpressed resentments and grudges are emotionally consuming and totally drain our present loving energy.

Writing blesses you with a literary Land Rover that can travel all terrains of hurt and anger. Through poetic remembrance, heart-to-heart talks, and compassionate notes, you can relive and revise some of your past harmful experiences. Poetry conveys love eloquently and is often used to soften our own struggles and those of our loved ones. Sincere, genuine written tokens of affection that we can offer our fellow travelers just might be the essential ingredient needed to heal their many hurts and struggles, but it also blesses our own hesitant journey during times of trouble. Each time we focus our attention on the joy and healing of another, our personal well-being is enhanced.

Giving is more empowering than taking. The more you give of yourself, the more you have to give. This is the secret to understanding tireless individuals. They're energized by giving, helping and loving other people. Why? Because giving creates abundance, whereas taking promotes scarcity. It's just a Law of the Universe.

Get your pen ready. Delight in the sheer, unadulterated, gut-wrenching, heart-rending, hair-ripping, nail-clenching power of the written word! It's the ultimate driving machine! Authored heartfelt words are seductive and heighten your partner's sexual sensitivities. Just as music moves the body, words move the soul. Gods and Goddesses of love melt and long for love notes. Write a poem, a love letter or a note that perfectly expresses your loving feelings and leave it, neatly printed or penned (not typed or hacked out on the computer), on any of the following:

→ his/her pillow

→ the refrigerator

→ the bathroom mirror

→ the steering wheel of the car

→ flowers

→ the dog's collar

→ a Single's Ad addressed specifically to your lover (yes, you'll have to point it out)

→ over the TV screen

→ his/her desk at work

→ in the underwear drawer

→ his/her bed

→ recite the poem in person as a singing telegram

→ record yourself and put the cassette in your lover's car

E ASY LIKE SUNDAY MORNING

Sunday morning. Want to know the secret messages of morning habits? The first thing we do after we wake up actually says a lot about who we are.

Do you:

1. Throw on your sneakers and go jogging (or pop in an aerobics video)?

2. Cuddle up to your mate for several minutes before getting out of bed?

3. Roll over and light a cigarette?

4. Make a beeline for the shower?

5. Read the paper or watch the morning news?

6. Lie in bed for several minutes without falling back asleep?

If you answered:

1. You're self-disciplined—bravo! But perhaps you put too much pressure on yourself.

2. You crave reassurance that everything is okay in the world. But your need to feel safe may signal insecurity or anxiety.

3. You're a pessimist and may anticipate a stressful day.

4. You're positive and upbeat, but your desire to make a clean start may mean you're superstitious.

5. You're hardworking and have a need to be in the know, though you may be too determined.

6. You're creative, confident, and in tune with what your body wants.

When it comes right down to it, time is all we really have to give another person. It's our most valuable resource. Our time is our life. Spend quality time with your love; create intimacy. Some time facts follow:

1. Most couples spend less than 30 minutes a week sharing intimate feelings.

2. Most people's lovemaking sessions take less than 25 minutes.

3. Most couples leave lovemaking until the very end ot the day, when they're tired, preoccupied and spent.

Are you giving your lover leftovers? Do you give each other whatever time is "leftover" from the rest of your life? If you don't consciously put your mate at the top of your priority list, he or she will automatically drop you to the bottom of the list. It's a Rule of Nature: "People take for granted those who are closest to them." The best gift is the gift of yourself, your time and attention. That's what your lover really wants from you . . . more of you.

There are those who want love and can't find it, but love is present—always. It lives as we live. It is the essence that gives breath to our bodies and to our souls. Love is meant to be gentle, to be easy, and is never hurried. It is our comforting blanket of protection and is always a choice.

We live in a culture that tells us love is "out there" somewhere. If we earn the right income, drive the right automobile, have the right hair-style, and wear the clothing that's in fashion, *then* we are worthy to find love or have love find us. In contrast, please understand that love really does originate from within. In truth, our ability to give and re-ceive love is directly proportional to our ability to love ourselves. We alone have the opportunity as well as the responsibility to create the love we desire in our lives.

Unconditional love is most often a process of letting go of those ob-stacles that block love's expression. Letting go of those personal "speed bumps" such as fear and low self-esteem, lets love in, moment by mo-ment. We're almost home, we're nearing the end of the "yellow brick road." We've discovered that we do have a heart, we do have a brain, and we do have the courage to seek the love we desire. This is Heaven on earth!

LIVING, LOVING AND LEARNING

*In the end, I
think my greatest
concern will be:
How much real
love did I have
in my life? How
did I share
my love? Who
honestly loved
me? Whom did I
treasure? Whose
lives did I impact?
Did my life make
a difference to
someone else?
Did I make the
world a better
place? No matter
what, I'm positive
my chief concern
will be about how
I did or did not
fill my life on
earth with love.*

S WAY TO THE MUSIC AND GET THE SHOW ON THE ROAD

Life, just like love, is a dance. A joyous, rhythmic, energetic swirl of activity. Sometimes we're waltzing, comfortably-paced and elegant. Sometimes we're wild and free-flowing, moving but not touching. Sometimes we're doing the tango, sensuous and pulsing. Sometimes it's ballet, and sometimes it's square dancing! Even if it's the two-step or the jitterbug, dancing is a form of foreplay. Certain songs make you lose control and dance like a wild savage, while others have a way of making you sway your body seductively and sexually. Celebrate! Celebrate! Dance to the music!

> *Touch, Love—Cha-cha-cha. Work, Play—Cha-cha-cha.*
>
> *Laugh, Cry—Cha-cha-cha. Live, Learn—Cha-cha-cha.*
>
> *Give, Take—Cha-cha-cha. Kiss, Hug—Cha-cha-cha.*

Movement is the essence of life and it's also an integral part of love. Love, like movement, is always growing, changing, and expanding. Stop traffic and be a human billboard! Move and groove your body to the music; let it shout "I LOVE YOU" to your partner. Try it, it's exhilarating! Body language does communicate an incredible amount of information—it is the expression of love. Tune-in to your mate's body, tune-in to your own body. Discover what kind of music *you're* dancing to.